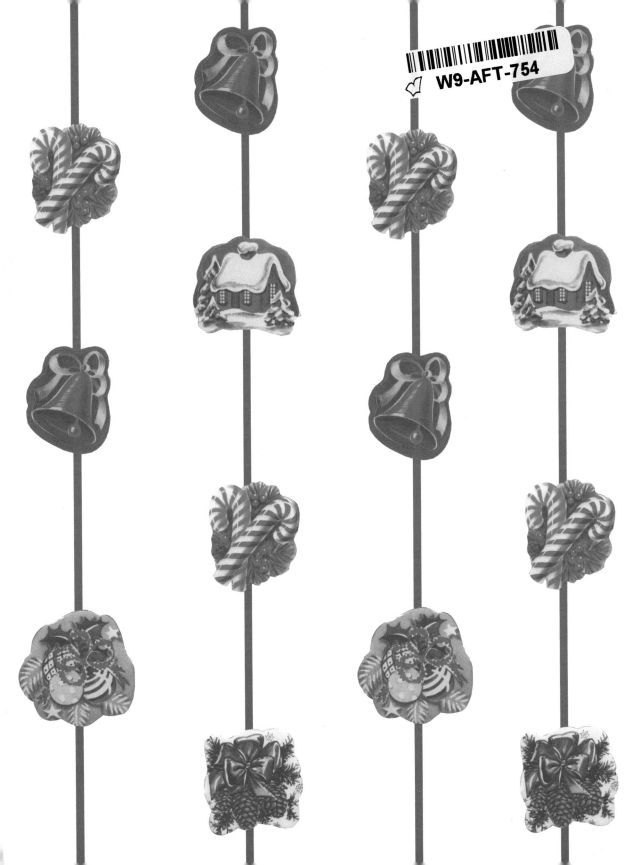

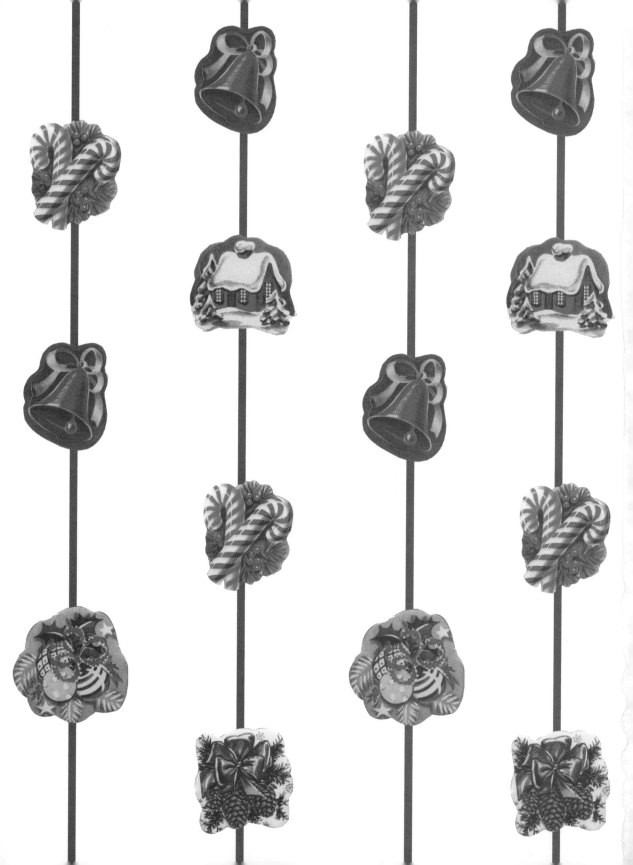

Christmas Memories

Christmas Memories

GIFTS, ACTIVITIES, FADS, AND FANCIES, 1920s–1960s

SUSAN WAGGONER

STEWART, TABORI & CHANG
NEW YORK

Published in 2009 by Stewart, Tabori & Chang
An imprint of ABRAMS

Library of Congress Cataloging-in-Publication Data

Waggoner, Susan.
  Christmas memories : gifts, activities, fads, and fancies, 1920s–1960s / Susan Waggoner.
    p. cm.
  ISBN 978-1-58479-789-0
  1. Christmas—United States—History—20th century. 2. United States—Social life and customs—20th century. I. Title.
  GT4986.A1W33 2009
  394.2663—dc22
                        2009011411

Editor: Dervla Kelly
Designer: Kay Schuckhart/Blond on Pond
Production Manager: Tina Cameron

The text of this book was composed in Adobe Caslon, Bodoni BE, and ValentinaJoy.

Printed and Bound in the United States
10 9 8 7 6 5 4

115 West 18th Street
New York, NY 10011
www.abramsbooks.com

Contents

THE 1920s
Jazz-Age Jubilee

Was there ever a decade in America that couldn't be described as a red-hot firecracker of a time? But the 1920s really lived up to the billing and during that decade Christmas, like everything else in America, began to shimmy and shake. Store windows sparkled and sometimes sang. Bright lights glittered on once-humble Main Streets. Some thought the excess signaled the end of the world. Others saw it as nothing more than the big, booming canvas of America itself.

Christmas in the Melting Pot

The decade that became known for its roar didn't start out that way. Costs had risen dramatically during World War I, but wages had not. After the war, poor business conditions and a significant decline in the stock market cast a further pall. Christmas of 1920 darkened retailer hearts with that most dreaded of all events—a buyers' strike. It was hardly an auspicious beginning. Yet, for many—the millions of immigrants who arrived early in the century—the future seemed bright.

On Christmas Eve of 1923, the SS *La Savoie* hovered just outside New York's harbor. Among those on board were Rozalia Bujaki and her five children, traveling from Hungary to join their husband and father in Detroit. Richard Bujaki, who heard the story of that night many times as he was growing up, recounts his father's first glimpse of the New World.

NEW YORK, DECEMBER 24, 1923

In their cabin aboard their steamship, my grandmother gathered her five children around her. My father, who was only seven at the time, watched as his mother opened the New Testament she had brought from home. This was the Christmas Story, printed in Hungarian, and he listened with his brothers and sisters as she read her favorite passages to them. When she finished, she reached into a bag and handed each child a single piece of fresh fruit. My father received an orange and, when nothing more was produced, felt a pang of disappointment. It was Christmas Eve. Like all children, he'd been hoping for a piece of candy. Looking up at his mother, he asked, "Is this all we get for Christmas?"

"No," his mother answered. "The best is yet to come."

Bundling up all of her children, she led them outside, onto the deck. In the cold night air, beneath a canopy of stars, she showed them the skyline of New York sparkling on the horizon. For the first time, my father saw the lights of the Woolworth Building, the tallest building in the world.

"Over there," his mother said, and pointed out the Statue of Liberty to them. "This is going to be your new home. It may be the greatest Christmas present you will ever receive."

My father wasn't impressed. He was cold, it was Christmas Eve, and he still wanted a piece of candy. Yet in the years that followed, this became his first and fondest recollection of Christmas in America.

—Richard Bujaki

The Christmas Look, Twenties Style

All Christmases are a pastiche of old and new, but none so much as those of the 1920s. America, especially in the first part of the decade, was of two minds: one that welcomed a world of accelerating change and one that still craved the comfort of the past. Both yearnings were reflected in the way Christmas looked. Nationwide, people gawked at the brightly lit trees and store windows on Main Street but questioned their appropriateness. Holly-sprigged tissue paper vied with geometrics worthy of Mondrian. On the family tree, drifts of old-fashioned angel hair fought it out with the spangly new gimcrack called tinsel.

Red and green lost the color war to primary colors, metallics, and shades of mint, lavender, robin's egg, faded rose, and other pastels. It's no accident that this was the decade that gave us pink poinsettias. Yet even as a distinctly American version of the holiday developed, the yearning for a simpler past continued its backward march— ultimately arriving at a Merrie Olde English–style Yuletide, which had never existed in America. Throughout the decade, the *Saturday Evening Post* satisfied both yens by alternating covers of dancing Victorians and London-bound mail coaches with Americanized toy shops and Santas.

Tree and Trim

Over the top didn't exist as a phrase in the 1920s, but if it had it would have aptly described Christmas trees of the era. Unlike later decades, which favored a pyramid-shaped tree tapering to a single point at the top, the Twenties demanded girth. The bigger around the middle the tree was, the better. If a tree grower could have cultivated a perfectly spherical tree, he would have made a fortune. Getting the desired girth often meant buying a tree much taller than the ceiling allowed, a tree that remained too tall even when the bottom branches were trimmed away. So the enterprising homeowner tackled the problem from the top; pictures from the era show

trees lopped off where they meet the ceiling, or the uppermost tips bent back.

Although tree lights had existed for some time, few family trees had them. For one thing, lights required electricity, something only about half of the population had. And even those who had electricity often found the lights too expensive—a string of colored lights in the early 1920s cost $3.50 (over $40 in contemporary dollars).

Yet even without lights, trees glittered. Tinsel, previously made of expensive silver, was now affordably mass-produced from inexpensive lead. Lametta garlands, with short, spiky strands bristling from the central wire, were especially popular, and came in shades of silver and gold.

Glass ornaments also added sparkle, though most trees—especially those of the early twenties—had fewer of them than trees of today typically do. Early ornaments had been expensive, with only one or two purchased by a family each year. In the 1880s, Woolworth's began importing less expensive glass ornaments from Germany, but the idea of a tree laden with balls had yet to take root. Such a tree would have struck many as a bit dull, since vying for space with glass ornaments were elaborate decorations made of paper. Heavyweight, embossed, artistically detailed, and printed in rich colors, these conveyed the sense of dizzying abundance that the era prized. If you examine a photo of a tree from this period, you'll see a fascinating and

multilayered mosaic. Paper ornaments knew no color scheme or season, nor was it uncommon to see seraphim mingling with crosses, lucky horseshoes, flowers, flags, Lady Liberties, harps, high-button shoes, fans, gloves, nosegays, and other motifs.

The finishing touch on the Twenties tree wasn't a star on top, as is popular today, but what sat beneath the lowest boughs. Although tree stands were available, they were not particularly stable and lacked water reservoirs, so many homeowners made their own arrangements. One of the fads of the time was to build a tiered box, insert the base of the tree in it, drape the box with fabric, and create miniature villages and landscapes in the snowy folds of material. Poring over old photos, we've spotted flocks of sheep, trains and trolleys, boats sailing beneath arched bridges, menageries of zebras and lions, ox carts, nativities flanked by camels and palms, and picket-fenced houses with lace curtains visible at the windows. One can only imagine the delight of the children for whom these tiny worlds came alive for a few weeks each year.

WAITING FOR THE TREE

Long after my sister and I were grown, my mother told us what her Christmases had been like growing up in the early 1920s. She told us that their house had pocket doors between the living room and the kitchen, and on Christmas Eve my grandfather would go into the living room, forbid anyone to bother him, and shut the doors behind him. About two hours later, when he opened the doors, the children were clustered there, waiting with impatient excitement. The living room was completely dark except for the tree Grandpa had miraculously snuck in and decorated with real lit candles on it. My mother said that every year, even though she knew what was coming, the candlelit tree was the most surprising, breathtaking thing she had ever seen. She told us this story the last year she was with us. It's a wonderful memory.

—Mary Ellen Timbs

Around the House

As in all decades, homes of the Twenties dressed up at Christmas and showed off the treasures dear to their owners' hearts—treasures that often had little practical or monetary value but were beloved nonetheless. One form of decoration would have seemed curious to modern eyes. A decade earlier, the Beistle Company of Pennsylvania, famous for paper decorations and party goods, became the first American company to perfect the technique of making honeycomb tissue. By the 1920s, honeycomb trees, starbursts, and garlands were being produced in eye-catching red and green, as well as gold- and silver-foil paper, and could be found even in the grandest of homes. By far the most popular item was the red honeycomb bell. Hung in a doorway or suspended from the center of the ceiling, with crepe paper streamers radiating around it, it was a bright banner proclaiming that Christmas had once again arrived. Today we think of such decorations as cheap and disposable, the stuff of bridal shows and school parties, but for many who grew up back then, the sight of a honeycomb bell opens the door to a vanished world.

Suddenly Santa

One of the most striking new faces of the 1920s was Santa Claus. Of course, a form of Santa had been on the scene for years, a European émigré who was thin, elderly, and somewhat dour. He traveled through the night alone, no reindeer in sight, delivering necessities to the poor and doing his best to remain anonymous. There was nothing even remotely American about him, but, like other immigrants, he changed to fit in. Clement Clarke Moore set things in motion when his poem, *A Visit from St. Nicholas* (or *The Night before Christmas*), appeared in a New York newspaper in 1823. Despite the poem's widespread popularity, many people lacked a clear image of Santa. Television didn't exist; newspaper and magazine illustrations were limited to black-and-white, or black and white with a single color added. And photography, invariably black-and-white, was of the grainy, murky sort that hardly lent itself to flights of fancy.

But with the new century, magazines began to print their covers in color, and as the century advanced, manufacturers used full-color illustrations to draw attention to their ads. Two American illustrators in particular, J. C. Leyendecker and Norman Rockwell, created the forerunner of the modern Mr. Claus. Both painted numerous Santas in the 1920s, for magazines as well as advertisements. Leyendecker's vision was a larger-than-life Santa, a man of large girth and undoubtedly high blood pressure, whose face was nearly as red as his suit. Rockwell, who did his first covers for *The Saturday Evening Post* when Leyendecker was still its leading cover artist, fell into step with the vision. Both men's Santas had flowing hair and beards, suits

trimmed in white fur, and wide, equatorial belts. Both Santas, unlike their European predecessors, operated in a world of children, dispensing toys for all rather than charity for only the poor. Neither Santa was grim in the European sense, yet neither was the carefree Santa that eventually became the American standard. Both Santas were men with a job to do—a happy job, to be sure, but one with enormous responsibilities. Leyendecker's Santa was deeply wrinkled and could appear harried and even a bit fierce. Rockwell's Santa was frequently depicted as hatless and balding, a Santa who showed human vulnerabilities like worry and exhaustion.

Yet, harried or hatless, the new Santa was an enormous hit with the public. If they'd had such things back then he surely would have been named one of the decade's most influential players. For as Santa's popularity grew, businessmen discovered that Santa had a secret talent: he could sell things. Santa began to appear in more and more ads, grace more and more signs, and to be featured on more and more packaging. Santa could move merchandise, especially merchandise marketed to children, and with each cry of "Ooh, look what Santa brought me!" his status as a mega-icon increased.

Gifts and Greetings of the 1920s
We Wish You a Merry Christmas

Until the 1920s, the Christmas card as we know it—the folded item that arrives in an envelope and fills you with guilt for not yet having sent yours out—was not the norm. Instead, people sent postcards with just enough space on the back to write "Season's Greetings from Betty Lou and Dave." Postcards were a model of efficiency. You did not have to labor over what to write to your friends, you did not have to suffer through their accounts of little Tommy putting a frog in mommy's handbag, and you did not have to spend more than a penny to send one. You got to enjoy the pretty pictures, let your friends know you were thinking of them, and enjoy the fact that they were thinking of you in return. As social systems go, it was darned near perfect.

But as economic conditions improved during the decade, the Christmas postcard began to seem a bit old hat. The big four of American cards and gift wraps—Hallmark, Gibson, American Greetings, and Norcross—had all come into existence between 1905 and 1915, and the competition must have been fierce. So, with customers a bit more financially secure, they turned their focus to cards and envelopes.

Christmas cards had been around since the nineteenth century, but early cards featured such un-Christmassy themes as flowers, wreaths, summer landscapes, lucky horseshoes, and shamrocks. The 1920s took a new direction and gave cards a fresh look by introducing themes that were associated with the winter season or specifically Christmas. Playing out the decade's penchant of looking both forward and back, cards frequently depicted scenes of a hundred years ago, showing ladies with muffs and bonnets, gentlemen in knee britches, and horse-drawn coaches. Silhouettes were also popular, but a modern touch was added by placing them against pastel landscapes. Art Deco influences abounded, with stylized curves and strong geometrics. None of it was meant to be realistic. It was meant to cheer the soul and delight the eye—and it did. From the middle of the decade on, the folded card became the preferred mailed greeting.

Gifts of the Season

Throughout the 1920s, gift-giving escalated from homemade treats given to a few, to manufactured items given to many. Far from being mere crass consumerism, it was also a useful way to gather up the many strands of human life and activity in America and give people a common, and hopefully joyful, experience. If England had been the capital of Christmas in the nineteenth century, America was making a strong bid to become its capital city in the twentieth. As far away as Japan, schoolchildren studying English were advised to give Christmas gifts as a way of understanding American democracy.

Thanks for the Christmas box. Especially enjoyed the steamed pudding. Mother sent aprons and other kitchen things. This brings Merry Christmas. P.S.: Publisher sent two Venetian glass bottles.

—Willa Cather, letter to a childhood friend,
December 27, 1921

The roar that made the decade famous, the roar of money, was barely a whisper at first. Most folks went about their lives as usual, hoping the high inflation of 1920 and the high unemployment of 1921 didn't get married and have a depression. They didn't.

Santa Claus' Daughter Gets The Best Time Of All

One of the great bull markets of all time was getting ready to break out of its pen, and by the end of 1921, those at the top were already swimming in a thick layer of cream. the *New York Times* declared the shoppers' strike officially dead, at least as far as Fifth Avenue was concerned. "Shoulder to shoulder, almost cheek to cheek, the band of Christmas shoppers surrounded the two sales girls at the counter and demanded attention," one story began. It went on to describe a couple who had driven a delivery truck to 34th Street and parked near Macy's. While the wife went inside to shop, the husband guarded the truck. They were on their third or fourth stop of the day, and had already acquired a Christmas tree and trimmings, doll carriage, sled, pogo stick, and rocking horse. But these people were pikers compared to shoppers on Fifth Avenue, where the most expensive item on offer was a Russian sable coat made of 131 perfectly matched skins, going for a mere $60,000 ($714,285.70 in today's dollars).

"I want some inexpensive gifts for a few friends," said a prominent lawyer's wife to a Fifth Avenue jeweler. In half an hour, she selected a diamond-studded cigarette holder for $250, a Dorine box for $60, a flat platinum watch for $1,200, and a pair of jade earrings for $175.

—The *New York Times*, December 25, 1921

In her thirty-minute spree at the jeweler's, the lawyer's wife spent the equivalent of $20,059.55 in today's dollars—$2,976.20 for the cigarette holder, $714.30 for the trinket box, $14,285.70 for the platinum watch, and a trifling $2,083.35 for the earrings.

Of course, it took a while for the diamond-studded carpet to roll across the country, but roll it did. Throughout the decade, material life improved for most people. The assembly-line method devised by Ford was adopted by other manufacturers, creating more jobs—and more secure jobs—than ever before. Another auto-industry invention also became commonplace: credit. Affordable as they were, cars were big-ticket purchases that would require many years of saving to afford. When car manufacturers realized it was to everyone's advantage to get cars into customers' hands as quickly as possible, the installment plan was born. Soon anyone with a steady income could enjoy owning a car as long as he made regular monthly payments on it.

He had tried to give her a ring for Christmas, and failing that, got her to accept a gold mesh bag that must have cost two hundred dollars.

—F. Scott Fitzgerald, "A Short Trip Home,"
The *Saturday Evening Post*, December 17, 1927

While only the very well-off could afford to give their dearly beloveds cars as gifts, the installment plan was also adapted to the burgeoning number of other consumer goods. Household appliances were popular gifts for women—toasters, vacuum cleaners, refrigerators, and washing machines especially. Far from seeing these gifts as impersonal and unromantic, the wives and mothers were delighted. Each item represented a palpable easing of drudgery, saving hours of time and labor. No matter what the appliance, the 1920s housewife had almost certainly never had anything like it. Also popular for women were gifts of jewelry. Wristwatches, originally called wristlets, had been created especially for women in the late nineteenth century and became increasingly popular. The young woman with a watch glittering on her wrist was busy and modern, with a full life and a schedule to meet. And if her timepiece drew attention to her finely turned wrist and pretty hands, all the better.

Since most men did not wear wristwatches until the mid-1920s, accessories for their pocket watches, such as fobs and chains, were more common as gifts early in the decade. Other popular choices for the men included stand-bys like pens, slippers, hats, ties, scarves, tools, and leisure-time items. America in those days was a country in which most men enjoyed fishing and hunting, both for recreation and for the food it added to the family larder. Rods and reels, shotguns, and hunting gear of any sort were all good bets. If the chap in question was the drinking sort, anything with a whiff of alcohol about it would do. Ironically, the Prohibition that was meant to eliminate the evils of drink caused a nationwide mania for it, and created a thriving subindustry of smuggling, counterfeiting, and concealing. Hip and pocket flasks to conceal contraband were fashionable, but even women came into consideration, and daintier flasks that could held in place by stocking garters were also made. Hardware stores even cashed in on the act by selling a special oil can. Who would ever guess that, hidden in plain sight among Dad's tools was an altogether different sort of lubrication? The most prized gift, of course, was alcohol itself—not the bruising bathtub variety, but the real thing, smuggled in from Canada. If you had the connections and could get the wholesale price, you could buy a case of Seagram's in the Midwest, just after it entered the country, for $35. By the time it got to Buffalo, it was $50. And in New York City, the same case went for $140 (in today's dollars, the equivalent of $142 a *bottle*)—and that was wholesale!

For children, classic toys were still the rule of the day—teddy bears, dolls, tea sets, story books, crayons and coloring books, balls, jump ropes, wagons, wind-up toys, sleds, scooters, and carts, and—as always for boys—just about anything with wheels. Undoubtedly, dolls were the most asked-for gifts for girls. Luckily, they came in a wide range of prices and sizes, so just about every girl could hope for one, from the popular but inexpensive Kewpie doll to the mid-range Raggedy Ann, to the pricey new girl on the block—the doll that said "mama." And if a little girl already had the doll of her dreams, there were still cradles and carriages to yearn for.

Some of the most popular toys with French shoppers this season are of American origin. Small boys in Parisian tam o'shanter and pinafore have been seen confiding to father that they would rather have the complete Indian suit with feathered headdress, tomahawk and beads than anything on display. With the cowboys' revolver, sombrero and chaps as a possible second.

—Herald Tribune, December 14, 1924

For most boys, electric trains were an item of breathless fascination, though many youngsters knew they could not hope for one. Even if their home had electricity, a simple set with an engine and a few cars was still quite expensive. Most boys were willing to settle for wooden or metal cars, tractors, and trains that could be pushed or pulled the old-fashioned way. Cowboy and Indian paraphernalia, toy soldiers, miniature farm sets, and building toys such as Lincoln Logs and Erector Sets were also popular. New to the scene was the pogo stick. Introduced at the beginning of the decade, it was an instant hit and soon became a nationwide craze.

The Cost of Christmas: 1920s

After 1921, inflation remained relatively low throughout the decade. This, combined with rising wages, a welter of new consumer goods, and the ability to buy on the installment plan, added to the era's sense of prosperity.

Equivalents in contemporary dollars, rounded to the nickel, are listed in parentheses.

"See How Big I Am" She's 27 in. tall—almost as big as the happy girls who will play with her. Has gorgeous long curls, beautiful blue eyes and real eyelashes. Sleeps and talks. Green organdy dress with matching green hair ribbon, undergarment, socks and slippers. Hard-to-break composition head, legs and arms. Strong stuffed body. G9J7760. Shipping wt., 6 lbs. . . $3.45

String of sixteen colored lights: $3.50 ($43.75)

Three sheets of decorated gift wrap: $.25 ($3.10)

Sweet Home chocolates, pound box: $.39 ($4.90)

Oreo cookies, per pound: $.35 ($4.40)

Dr. Swift's root beer, eight-ounce bottle: $.09 ($1.20)

Butter, per pound: $.55 ($6.70)

Sugar, five-pound bag: $.35 ($4.30)

Cranberry sauce, per can: $.24 ($3.00)

Beef rib roast, per pound: $.39 ($4.90)

Long Island duck, per pound: $.29 ($3.60)

Men's silk tie: $.47–$1.50 ($5.90–$18.75)

Men's felt hat: $3.85 ($48.10)

Mark Cross attaché case: $40.00–$50.00 ($500.00–$625.00)

Women's wristwatch: $5.00 ($62.50)

Wavette curling iron: $2.19 ($27.40)

Sloane vacuum cleaner: $48.00 ($600.00)

White Mountain refrigerator: $49.50 ($618.75)

Radio "having a range of five hundred miles and more": $23.50 ($293.75)

Victrola record player with mahogany stand: $75.00 ($937.50)

Record: $.39 ($4.90)

Sled: $3.75–$6.00 ($46.90–$75.00)

Cocker spaniel puppy: $20.00 ($241.95)

Toddler doll that walks and talks: $3.50 ($43.75)

Football: $1.95 ($24.40)

Electric train set: $7.50 and up ($89.30 and up)

Toy six-shooters in fringed artificial-leather holsters: $1.00 ($12.50)

Fishing rod and tackle set: $15.00 ($178.60)

Wrap It Up

Wrapping a package in the Twenties was no easy matter. In fact, it was a downright medieval endeavor full of setbacks and frustration. All for one simple reason—it was a world without Scotch tape. Hard to imagine, isn't it? To secure the wrapping paper and hold the ends in place, small seals were used. Usually about one-inch square, the tiny seals were gummed on one side while the other side sported colorful pictures—candles, poinsettias, snowmen, reindeer, and the like. (Christmas seals got their start this way, distributed as useful items that would remind people of the season's charitable aspects.) To secure your package, you had to lick the seal's gummed side, hold it in place until it stuck, and hope it didn't fall off while you were tying the ribbon on. Seals left over from last season had a tendency to dry out and curl up, making them especially difficult to work with.

The troublesome seals, however, were more than compensated for by the gift wrap of the era. Elaborate paper was still a new item. In the past, gifts had been wrapped in tissue paper, either plain red or green, or white with a pattern of holly springs. Then, one day in 1917, the Hallmark store ran out of tissue at the height of the Christmas rush and offered paper meant to be used as envelope liners as a substitute. The paper, beautifully decorated and heavier than the tissue, was a huge success. The next year Hallmark sold the decorated sheets alongside traditional tissue, much to customers' delight. Other companies soon emulated Hallmark's success. Wrapping paper of the 1920s was quite luxurious. It often came in coordinated sets with embossed seals, gift tags, and tasseled cord. Many papers were foiled, or incorporated metallic elements into the design. Strong tones— deep crimson, lapis lazuli, bronze, and even black-and-white— were popular, as were geometric patterns such as diamonds,

squares, and plaids. Modern gift wrap—or gift dressing, as it was then called—had been born, and became a well-established staple of the holiday season.

Ain't We Got Fun

Until its abrupt fall in the final months of 1929, the 1920s was a decade of dizzying growth and forward motion. While few people became rich, most became richer than they had been. The sense of prosperity, combined with new entertainments and conveniences, cast a glow over life in general and the holidays in particular. In the city, tree-trimming parties—meant to show off the hosts' strings of colored electric bulbs—became fashionable. The wealthy had an even newer toy, the midwinter holiday. Europe was a popular destination, as it had been in the nineteenth century, but new destinations were also springing up closer to home. "Fleets are in readiness to transport the winter vacationist from the frozen North to lands of eternal summer," the *Literary Digest* promised in a December 18, 1926 article, going on to describe the delights of Bermuda, Nassau, Cuba, Jamaica, and other islands of the West Indies and Caribbean.

Even for those of modest and limited means there were new amusements to be had. In 1923, a Christmas tree, complete with lights, appeared on the White House lawn for the first time. Several thousand people turned out to watch. Other cities followed suit, decorating Main Streets and town squares with lights, wreaths, and greenery. For many people, electricity was still a novelty, and whether the tree was on the White House lawn or in the public square of their own small town, it was worth venturing out to see. Going downtown became a popular pastime, and stores made sure there was plenty on view. These were the days before national chains, when Marshall Field's was as Chicago as Chicago could be, and *Does Macy's tell Gimbels?* was more than just a phrase. Hoping to garner holiday sales, stores did everything they could to draw customers, from creating windows that told elaborate stories to sponsoring contests to holding parades that ended, by pure circumstance, at the store's main entrance.

Let's Have a Parade!

And I was told there was no religion in America. Even on Corpus Christi we didn't have such processions in Slovenia.

—Marie Prisland

For most immigrants, Christmas was a link between the Old World and the New. Many of the traditions were familiar, and those that weren't were embraced with all the more enthusiasm for being American. In return, the new arrivals incorporated their own traditions into the broad mainstream of their new lives and it was the longing for one tradition in particular that gave the country one of its most famous "American" events.

In the early 1920s, many Macy's employees were foreign-born residents, who shared memories of the traditional processions that marked European festivals. Wanting to celebrate both their new lives and their old, they asked the store's president, Herbert Strauss, if they could put on a parade marking the holiday season. Strauss warmed to the idea instantly. Macy's, long famous for its holiday windows, had just added a Seventh Avenue wing, making it "the World's Largest Department Store." Why not celebrate the holidays and express gratitude for the store's success with a parade that would lead customers right to the door?

Advertised as "a surprise New York will never forget," the first parade (known as Macy's Christmas Parade until the 1930s), stepped off smartly on November 27, 1924. It included four marching bands, Mother Goose characters atop horse-drawn floats, hundreds of Macy's employees dressed as clowns, cowboys, knights, and sheiks, and over two dozen camels, elephants, donkeys, and goats from the Central Park Zoo. When Santa's sleigh arrived at the end of the procession, a trumpet was sounded and, at Santa's signal, the holiday windows were unveiled.

For once, reality more than lived up to the hype, and the big surprise became even bigger in subsequent years. Lions and tigers from the zoo were added but when the beasts frightened children and aroused safety concerns, the store found a creative substitute—giant balloons. In 1927 Felix the Cat became the first floating celebrity to wend his way down Broadway.

A Night at the Algonquin, 1927

The same electricity that made brightly lit windows and electrified trees a novelty also powered another amusement of the era—radio. Though still too expensive for most families, those who had them were treated to a fare of sermons, carols, holiday recipes, and, of course, the ever-popular holiday special.

In December of 1927, in what must have seemed a surefire bid to make the season of cheer all the cheerier, programmers at NBC's radio network decided to create a very special Christmas memory—a live broadcast from New York's Algonquin Hotel, featuring the wits of the famous Round Table. Luring the participants with promises of complimentary cocktails and unlimited pierogi (booze and food always being a draw with writers, starving or otherwise), they set the table and waited for genius to take hold. Among the moths fluttering to the flame were wisecracking poet Dorothy Parker, playwright George S. Kaufman (author of *Animals Crackers*, *The Coconuts*, and *A Night at the Opera*), tartly witty columnist and theater critic Alexander Woollcott, and satirists Robert Benchley and Franklin Pierce Adams. Regrettably, no one seemed to have alerted the participants to the presence of live microphones or reminded them that it was, after all, Christmas. As was their custom, the assembled members looked around, noted who was absent, and began trashing those not present with bright-eyed enthusiasm. Thus was America's fledgling radio audience treated to a number of scintillating attacks on Edna Ferber's recently published *Mother Knows Best*. As libations continued to flow, the conversation became even more freewheeling, turning to the more pressing matter of how dreary, frustrating, and generally lacking the members' sex lives were. NBC continued the experiment for almost half an hour, pulling the plug only after Dorothy Parker, accepting another cocktail, quipped, "One more of these and *I'll* be sliding down Santa's chimney."

Good-bye to All That

Address: 1600 Pennsylvania Avenue, N.W.,

detached brick, covered with stucco.

Occupant: Herbert C. Hoover.

First alarm box 157, 8:09 P.M., 24 December

—Report of Fire Marshal C. G. Achstetter,
7:27 A.M., 25 December 1929

The fun, of course, came to an end in October of 1929. So it was only fitting that the year ended, quite literally, in flames. In the White House, President Hoover and his wife were hosting a party for members of the president's staff and their families in the State Dining Room. Refreshments had been served, presents handed out, and games begun when the president's personal secretary informed him that a fire had broken out in the East Wing.

Leaving his wife and the Marine Band to keep the party going, the president, his son, and his aides hurried to the fire. According to newspaper accounts, President Hoover attempted to join in fighting the fire himself but was held back by his aides. Although the police and fire departments were quick to respond, it took some hours to completely extinguish the fire. Damage amounted to $135,000 (approximately $1.7 million in today's dollars). All in all, it had been one heck of a decade.

WOMAN'S WORLD

DECEMBER · 1933   10 CENTS A COPY

"AHASUERUS AND ESTHER" by AGNES SLIGH TURNBULL

The Romance of a King

The Best of Times In the World of Times

It was by all accounts one of the bleakest decades in American history. You'd think Christmas would be cancelled, wouldn't you? But it wasn't. Instead, people seemed to enjoy it all the more for the hard times they endured. The Yuletide spirit burned bright, even if the gifts were poorer and the plates less full. In fact, some of the very traditions we think of today as emblems of the big, rosy, plush-lined modern Christmas got their start in the hardest of hard times.

After the Fall

On October 29, 1929, the stock market still managed to close at 230.7, far above the low of 41.22 that would take another two-and-a-half years to reach. Not everyone felt the pinch of hard times right away, but for those who lost their jobs early on, the fall was swift and hard. Unemployment insurance did not exist, and few people had enough to live on their savings.

THE GREEN WAGON

In 1963, in a piece for the *Detroit Free Press*, Damon Keith wrote about being a child during the early days of the Great Depression. In 1928, the family had been happy and secure. His father, a Ford Motors employee, had easily been able to afford a Christmas gift for each of his children. Keith's gift had been a shiny green wagon. By Christmas 1929, the wagon, battered from use and missing a wheel, sat on the porch.

Despite the fact that his father had lost his job, Keith and his siblings asked Santa for gifts just as they always had. When Christmas Eve arrived, Keith's father took him by the hand and the two walked several blocks to a neighborhood hardware store. Here, for ten cents, his father bought a new wheel for the green wagon. This, his father explained, was all there was money for this year.

Keith vividly remembered the walk home through the frosty air. "As we left the store and started our walk home," he wrote, "my father discussed, in his quiet, simple, but dignified manner, what Christmas meant to him. He said that we as a family should be thankful to God for the food on our table, the roof over our heads, that God had allowed us to be together for another year without a link in our family chain being broken, and that He had blessed us with good health and we as a unit had the love that Christmas stood for."

Christmas Greetings

Keith went on to become a lawyer, a co-chairman of the Michigan Civil Rights Committee, and a judge of the U.S. Sixth Circuit Court of Appeals. He wrote that he never forgot that night, that gift, or the lesson he learned. It was a lesson many families would learn over the next decade, in a depression that lasted longer and ran deeper than anyone could have imagined.

The Christmas Look, Thirties Style

In the 1930s, America was swept with a wave of nostalgia for the world of Charles Dickens, possibly because his plucky orphans and sly survivors mirrored the spirit of the Great Depression. At the other end of the spectrum was swank late-phase Art Deco, which could be seen everywhere but in the decorations themselves, which remained traditional. The biggest change that came with the Thirties was the use of color. Exit the subdued pastels of the 1920s, enter bright, solid colors and the triumph of vibrant, traditional red and green.

Tree and Trim

For most people, the Christmas tree remained the one must-have of the holiday season, to be decorated in the grandest style possible. The paper ornaments of yesterday had become a bit shabby by now, not only worn but outdated as well. But tinsel and ornaments remained in style, and thanks to Woolworth's most people could afford at least a few items to make the tree sparkle.

Woolworth's began importing inexpensive ornaments from Germany in the 1880s and now both Japan and Czechoslovakia entered the market. Most people could afford at least a few purchased ornaments and supplemented store-bought sparkle with paper chains, garlands of popcorn and cranberries, and other homemade decorations.

1931: WE HAVE $12.73

We can't afford the made-in-Japan splendors at the five-and-dime. So we do what we've always done: sit for days at the kitchen table with scissors and crayons and stacks of colored paper. I make sketches and my friend cuts them out: lots of cats, fish too (because they're easy to draw), some apples, some watermelons, a few winged angels devised from saved-up sheets of Hershey bar tin foil. We use safety pins to attach these creations to the tree; as a final touch, we sprinkle the branches with shredded cotton (picked in August for this purpose). My friend, surveying the effect, clasps her hands together. "Now honest, Buddy. Doesn't it look good enough to eat?"

—"A Christmas Memory," Truman Capote

Although electricity remained an expensive luxury for many and most rural areas still lacked service, improvements in technology and design made tree lights more appealing than ever. Strings used less electricity, burned-out bulbs could more easily be replaced, and beads and clips helped keep the lights in place. Shapes also became more fanciful. There were bell-shaped lights, faceted cones, and rosettes and stars in which

the bulb was surrounded by points of glass or metal. But the biggest innovation, which would become a permanent part of Christmas, was tie-ins to popular characters in the culture. Cartoon characters were especially popular, and bell lights with decals of Mickey and Minnie Mouse, the Katzenjammer Kids, and Popeye and his gang were all produced during this decade.

ON THE BERING SEA, 1932

I know you would like to know what kind of decorations we have here at Hooper Bay. Well, we used a lot of that crepe paper they use for making flowers. We made rings, twisted different colors together, made little lanterns, and other little things. Besides that, we used some of those festoons some kind benefactor sent to us.

—Novice Nun, Sisters of Our Lady of the Snows Mission,

Hooper Bay, Alaska

EDISON MAZDA LAMPS
GENERAL ⊕ ELECTRIC

60 watt
Edison MAZDA Lamp

Edison MAZDA
Flame Tint Lamp

MAZDA Photoflash
Lamp

MAZDA Sunlight
Lamp (Type S-2)

Light Up...for a Happier Holiday

LET your home typify the Christmas spirit. Light it cheerfully with Edison MAZDA* Lamps.

And when the children gather around the tree, use Edison MAZDA Photoflash Lamps to take their pictures. What memories for future years! Anyone can take flashlight pictures by using Edison MAZDA Photoflash Lamps.

A fixture using the new MAZDA Sunlight Lamp (Type S-2) will bring the benefits of ultra-violet radiation into your home at small cost. Children need this Vitamin D building radiation, which helps to promote the growth of strong bones and teeth. Look for the name EDISON on the carton and MAZDA and ⊕ on the bulb.

*MAZDA—the mark of a research service.

Santa on a Roll

The popularity of Santa Claus, firmly established in the Twenties, continued to grow through the Thirties. In the 1920s, Coca-Cola had begun advertising during the holiday season in an effort to promote their soft drink as something to be drunk year-round and not simply during the summer. One of the ads featured a department-store Santa enjoying the drink. In the early 1930s, the company commissioned illustrator Haddon Sundblom to develop images of Santa that could be used in their ads. When Sundblom's first ad premiered in 1931, the modern Santa had come into his own. Like the Santa depicted by Leyendecker and Rockwell in the 1920s, Sundblom's Santa was a man of very large girth, dressed in a red suit and sporting a mane of white hair. Yet this Santa, despite his age, was very much like the children he served. Gone were the lines of worry and age. Santa now had a twinkle in his eye and a merry smile, and he wasn't above pausing to play with the toys as he arranged them under the tree. The vision of Santa as a man in touch with his inner boy was an immediate success, and quickly became the standard interpretation.

The Sundblom Santa was far more child friendly than earlier Santas and set the stage for Santa's reign as a retail icon. Increasingly, he stepped out of storybooks and advertisements and became a living figure, at least for a few weeks each year. Although Santa had been used to attract children into store toy departments before, the trend went big in the Thirties. Soon no self-respecting town was without at least one store where Santa held court, sitting on a thronelike chair as children lined up to tell him their Christmas wishes. If the store was large, he often occupied his own special Toy Town within it, with elves to attend him as he went about his business. Before the decade was out, the men in red had formed their own national association, and the first school for professional Santas had opened. Over the course of a week, prospective Santas learned salesmanship and showmanship, got instructed in the ups and downs of child psychology, and were brought up to date on the season's most desirable toys. During the 1930s, Santa was a one-man WPA, employing thousands of men at relatively good wages, if only for a few weeks a year.

Gifts and Greetings of the 1930s
Wishing You All Good Things

Coming home late one evening, her arms piled high with packages, a lady we know saw a weary little postman stop his truck at a corner mailbox. He had to make two trips to empty it of its brimming loads of Christmas greetings. Finally he slammed the door of the box shut, locked it, and then said to it, in a tone of quiet desperation, "I hate you."

—The *New Yorker*, December 23, 1939

People did not stop sending cards during the Depression, or even revert to the less expensive Christmas postcard. Instead, the postcard continued to fade from the scene, and soon vanished altogether, while cards grew more imaginative than ever before. To be sure, there were many who may have sent homemade cards, or written letters on a new product on the market—stationery decorated with Christmas motifs and themes—but purchased cards remained the most common way of saying "Merry Christmas," especially in an era when phone calls to those even a few miles away could be expensive long-distance affairs.

Cards of the era embraced a broad range of motifs. English country themes were still popular, though the colors were bolder and brighter. The Art Deco influence, still in evidence early in the decade, was gradually replaced by a more realistic style. Many cards reflected the longing for a happy, secure world—glamorous women shopping and putting up wreaths as if they'd never heard the word *Depression*,

TO MY WIFE
There's no argument about it
I wish you a Very
MERRY CHRISTMAS!

houses drowsing under blankets of snow, cozy fireplaces, and cheerful pups abounded. Scottish terriers were especially popular, no doubt since Fala, FDR's Scottie, was a White House resident. Overtly religious themes were more popular than they had been in the past while, at the other end of the spectrum, some designers abandoned traditional Christmas themes and offered cards showing secular winter activities, such as skiing. Many cards were humorous, making lighthearted fun of the Depression and, until it ended in 1933, Prohibition.

Ever-innovative Hallmark licensed the use of both Popeye and Disney characters and embellished their cards with eye-catching extras such as ribbon, foil, glitter, and flocking. New to the scene was the personalized card, preordered and printed with the sender's name, while celebrities often designed their own limited edition cards.

Last week in Manhattan there was an exhibition of Christmas cards, at the Hotel New Weston, and some people observed that it was far more in the spirit of Rome than Bethlehem. Britain's Royal Family always choose large, colorful, spirited Christmas cards. New York's Bishop William Thomas Manning had one of the few pious greetings in the exhibition. Cinema and stage folk run to large, expensive Christmas cards, with heavy silver paper and fancy typography. Alla Nazimova sends her signature, in red ink. Lily Pons puts a picture of herself in a folder of heavy silver paper, wrapped in cellophane. Eddie Cantor caricatures his large eyes, surrounded by holly wreaths. Helen Morgan sits on a piano, weeping and singing. George Gershwin caricatures his profile. John P. Morgan, Anne Morgan, Noel Coward, Calvin Coolidge, Mrs. Vincent Astor were asked for cards for the exhibit, replied that they had none to exhibit this year.

—*Time*, December 12, 1932

Gifts of the Season

My Dear Mrs. Roosevelt,

Only Our Maker knows how happy I could be if at Christmastime I could have a loan or a personal gift of say $100 or even more so I could get a radio, and a good bed or two and some bed covering, warm clothes for children and husband, and a piece of furniture or two for living room, some paint and curtains, etc. and have a pretty little tree with toys, and have my teeth fixed. We have worked so hard and yet it seems as if we are getting lower and lower.

Mrs. Mona Smith

Batavia, Ohio, December 1, 1937

Gifts during the 1930s focused on the practical—clothes, personal items, toys that would not break or bore quickly, and anything that could be shared with others. It was a time when people did not pin their big hopes for the year on the holiday. New socks or slippers, a pretty tablecloth, a tin of pipe tobacco, something made by hand and given with love—for most adults, these gifts were enough. Homemade gifts were especially common in this decade—aprons, monogrammed hankies, embroidered dresser scarves, and pillow cases were all given and received with appreciation for the time that went into them.

That didn't mean people totally put aside their wishes, though. Heading into the Christmas season of 1938, Kaufmann's department store in Pittsburgh asked customers what gift they would like if cost were no object. The gift most often named by men was a car. Second choice among young men was a house, the exception being a young man who wanted a diving suit.

Older men gave second place to cash, world cruises, boats, diamond studs, and a paid-up mortgage. Most women, regardless of age, put a fur coat at the top of the list, with a car in second place. Other objects of feminine desire were a large emerald, airplane, rug, horse, model kitchen, piano, and Clark Gable—not necessarily in that order.

The one gift a family might consider splurging on during the decade was a radio. In the Twenties, the appliance was considered so expensive that radio tubes, rather than radios themselves, were advertised as affordable gifts. By the Thirties, however, manufacturers were making less expensive tabletop models, a streamlining much like going from the living room console stereo of the 1960s to the boom box of later years. Penny for penny, the radio was the news and entertainment buy of the century, carrying everything from farm and weather reports in the morning to soap operas during the day and dramas, mysteries, comedies, and quiz shows at night, with the president's Fireside Chats thrown in as a bonus. Not to have a radio was to live in gray isolation, to put your children at a disadvantage at school, and to find yourself out of the loop when people made jokes about Fibber McGee's closet.

The radio told you what was on sale downtown, provided recipes and household hints, and kept you informed about events around the world. More than any other single item, the radio, even if it had to be paid for in installments, made the unbearable Depression easier to bear.

Most parents preferred to do with less in the way of gifts so their children could have more, and for tots there was plenty to want. The introduction of the DyDee doll in 1933, the first doll to drink and wet, blazed a trail of desire though the under-ten crowd. DyDee was quickly followed by other big-name dolls, including Shirley Temple and Betsy Wetsy (1934), the Dionne Quintuplets (1935), Snow White (1937), and Little Lulu (1939). For girls whose parents couldn't afford dolls, there were paper dolls, as well as doll clothes, handmade by mother, to give last year's doll a new look. Dollhouses, either store-bought or made by dad, were also popular, and dime stores carried inexpensive cardboard furniture to cut out and paste together.

December 6, 1931

Dear Santa,

I thought as Christmas is not so very long off, I had better write you. I want you to please bring me a string of beads and a ring. Also bring me lots of fruits, nuts, and candy. Don't forget the orphans and my little friend, Dave. I think he wants a billy goat, a wagon, and a pair of pajamas, so he won't get so cold.

I am your little girl,
Ruby Baucom
Malakoff, Texas

For boys, the focus remained on trains, which grew more elaborate with every year. Lionel even added a steam whistle, a miniature of the real thing. Bicycles, cars, trucks, and building toys remained popular, as did footballs, boxing gloves, bats and balls, and the new craze, yo-yos. Roller skates and sleds were popular for both boys and girls, as were items associated with popular figures from radio, the movies, cartoons, and comics, such as Little Orphan Annie, Flash Gordon, and Hopalong Cassidy. From Shirley Temple necklaces to Dick Tracy pencil cases, the glitter of celebrity made young hearts glad.

Games were extremely popular, since they could be shared and enjoyed for hours at a time. Chinese checkers, which were introduced at the very end of the 1920s, as well as traditional checkers, were popular, as were card games. Board games became a particular craze, especially Sorry!, introduced in 1934, followed the next year by the game that was to become the best-selling board game of all time, Monopoly.

For younger children of both sexes, one of most frequently given gifts was one you'll never see in a toy catalogue of the era. Humble and homemade, the sock monkey was the unsung toy of the Depression. The stage was set at the turn of the century, when Nelson Knitting Mills began making their brown-and-white work socks with a distinctive red crescent heel. It wasn't long before some enterprising home crafter realized you could made a very nice stuffed animal from the socks, strategically cutting them to make the crescent into the monkey's mouth. Other stuffed animals were also created, but none was quite as popular. The Nelson Company began including instructions with the socks in the 1920s, and it's impossible to calculate how many of the whimsical creatures were crafted in the decades that followed. One of the most appealing things about the toy monkey was that it never seemed a stand-in for something else. Each monkey was unique, male or female, young or old, silly or wise, sporting overalls or frills, its face reflecting an individual who could not be duplicated by any machine for any amount of money.

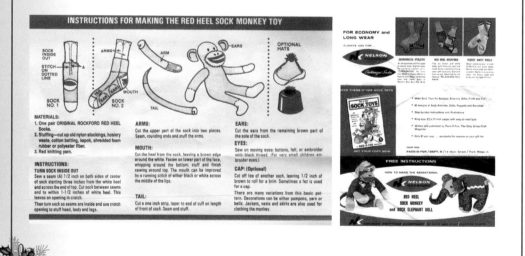

Our house and connecting Radio and Music store were on Main Street in Dennisport, a tiny Cape Cod village. Dad put colored lights on the ever-greens outside and in the store windows, and played Christmas music through a loudspeaker for shoppers to hear all over Main Street.

He spent Christmas Eve delivering new radios all over Cape Cod and didn't get home until nearly midnight. By 5:00 A.M. Christmas morning we were clamoring to see if Santa had come. Dad said we must wait till Mother was seated and he had stoked the stove for warmth. At last, he unhooked our bedroom door and we rushed into the living room and saw the lighted tree.

We'd left out the long tan stockings we wore to school in winter. Now they were lumpy with shiny pennies and lovely oranges in the toe, and boxes of new crayons, drinking bottles for our dolls, walnuts in the shell, and big peppermint candy canes. Santa left each of us three girls a DyDee doll that drank and wet her diaper. There were tiny clotheslines, and clothespins for the flannel dolls' diapers. Dad made us a dollhouse from a wooden crate, with a peaked roof and three shelves in it, so we could each have a shelf of our own. The dollhouse was painted with leftover brown paint. Wow! We had a dollhouse.

Santa brought our brother a bouncing horse he could ride and a new red wagon. He got Lincoln Logs and Tinkertoys and a group of house parts he could fit together to make six-inch-high houses. We also got a toy typewriter. We'd turn a wheel and print one letter at a time. We were happy, for now we could put out our own newspaper of family happenings. It took forever to do it and it kept us busy for many hours that winter.

Nana and Grampa Dean came for Christmas turkey dinner and stayed all after-noon to watch us with our wonderful presents. Dad put up the card table and we worked together on a jigsaw puzzle. By the end of the day, we were tired and ready for bed early. We took our new dolls with us, and our brother took his new teddy bear. We'd had an amazing Christmas.

—Betty Dean Holmes

The Cost of Christmas: 1930s

Prices generally were in a deflationary spiral throughout the 1930s, with some groceries the cheapest they'd been in fifteen years—little comfort for those whose wages had fallen even further.

Equivalents in contemporary dollars, rounded to the nickel, are listed in parentheses.

Oysters, per quart: $.55 ($7.74)

Prime rib roast, per pound: $.18 ($2.55)

Ham, per pound: $.39 ($6.40)

California oranges, per dozen: $.21 ($3.45)

Banana split at a soda fountain: $.15 ($2.50)

Carton of Camel cigarettes, in holiday wrap: $1.75 ($24.65)

Christmas tree, six feet tall: $2.50 ($35.20)

Women's silk stockings, per pair: $.89 ($12.55)

Women's camel hair and Shetland tweed coat: $18.95 ($278.70)

Men's suit: $17.75 ($268.95)

Men's Arrow shirt: $2.00 ($30.80)

Electric iron: $1.49 ($23.30)

Emerson five-tube bedroom radio: $9.95 ($150.75)

Shaefer pen: $3.35 and up ($47.20 and up)

Movie ticket, national average: $.23 ($3.50)

Piedmont & Northern Railroad holiday special fare, per mile: $.04 ($.55)

Dinner at the Moose Grill, Waldorf Astoria, New York, per person: $2.00 ($31.25)

Sled with steering mechanism: $.98 ($15.30)

Sears bicycle: $19.95 ($316.65)

Clamp-on adjustable roller skates, per pair: $.69 ($10.60)

"Farm for Sale" toy farm with buildings and animals: $1.00 ($14.70)

Mechanized toy tractor that "will climb over most anything": $1.34 ($21.95)

Two pairs of boys' sheepskin boxing gloves: $1.89 ($27.80)

Plastic G-Man pistol that shoots sparks of light: $.44 ($6.50)

African-American walking doll, eighteen inches tall: $.89 ($13.05)

You should have no hesitancy in equipping yourself to put this product on the market economically. There will be a sufficient volume of sales to justify the expenditure.

—Letter to 3M from a prospective customer, after testing Scotch tape

See You in the Funny Papers

Wrapping paper was sold throughout the 1930s, but during the hard years of the Depression people often dispensed with it as an unnecessary expense. The less expensive tissue paper of old was used, or paper that had been used before and carefully smoothed and saved. The funny papers were always a good bet, and regular white or brown paper could be decorated with gummed stars and pictures cut from magazines. And if the paper wasn't quite as good as it had been in better times, the technology was better than ever—in 1932, 3M introduced Scotch tape, much to the delight of gift wrappers everywhere. During this era, people also economized by wrapping packages in useful items—a box of stationery might be wrapped in a hand-embroidered tea towel, a new pipe tucked into a pair of socks and tied with a bow. Greeting cards saved from past holidays could be turned into gift tags with a snip of the scissors. People might not have had a lot of money, but there was plenty of creativity to go around.

The Dazzle of It All

For a decade knocked flat on its back, the Thirties saw an amazing amount of *doing*. The Empire State Building was constructed in just a year and six weeks. Movies became larger than life, and blossomed with color. Millions of Americans pulled up stakes, moved thousands of miles, and started all over again. Christmas was celebrated in the same spirit, with activities and entertainment taking precedence over gifts.

In New York, despite the Fifth Avenue Association's attempt to suppress noise and showy displays with its "no motion in windows" edict of the 1920s, merchants redoubled their efforts to gussy up the holidays. Lord & Taylor ran afoul of the Association by staging an artificial blizzard in one of its windows. Then, far from hanging its head in shame, the store ignored the scolding it received and put Christmas bells in another window. Even worse was the dime store down the street, which featured

WOMAN'S WORLD

Merry Christmas

MIRIAM
STORY
HURFORD

December, 1930   "Devoted to the Better Things of Life"   15 Cents a Copy

Special Features by Nina Simmonds Estill - Sadie P. Le Sueur

mechanized tableaux, and the fur salon that had the temerity to put up an electrically lit sign apprising customers of a sale.

Fret though the Association might, the line had been crossed early in the decade, several years before these insurrections of light and noise took place. Around 1932, New York threw in the towel and decided to make a public spectacle of itself. By unspoken agreement, it decided to do Christmas big.

The center of the hubbub was the few blocks along Fifth Avenue from Forty-eighth to Fifty-first Streets, stretching west to Sixth Avenue. The land had been slated for a complex of buildings, including an opera house to be built by John D. Rockefeller Jr. in partnership with the Metropolitan Opera. When the market crash of 1929 forced the Metropolitan to withdraw, Rockefeller continued as the sole financier. Work on Rockefeller Center, the largest privately financed development in history, began in May of 1930 and took most of the decade to complete. The new design, sans opera house, featured an open promenade gracefully descending from the Fifth Avenue side, surrounded by a complex of more than a dozen commercial buildings. The project, jammed into the busy heart of one of the busiest cities in the world, became a tourist draw even when it was little more than a hole in the ground. Workmen, glad to have work to see them through the hard times, erected a twelve-foot white spruce on the construction site. In 1933, a much larger tree was erected and a public lighting ceremony held. The idea of a towering evergreen scaled to match the city's skyline was an immediate hit with the public, and the moment when the tree was lit became an event no one wanted to miss.

At the other end of the complex, on the Sixth Avenue side, Radio City Music Hall was completed at the tail end of 1932. The grand opening, held two days after Christmas, featured Ray Bolger, Martha Graham, and countless other acts. The idea was to bring classy, old-style variety-show entertainment back to the modern stage. The problem was that the stage was enormous—almost fifty yards wide. The performers were dwarfed by it and the audience, having become accustomed to larger-than-life entertainment at the movies, was having none of it. So the stage was fitted with a screen and the space reinvented as a movie palace. But one act, it was thought, still might work between shows: a line of high-stepping ladies who'd performed on opening night. Previously known as the Roxyettes, the troupe was rechristened the Rockettes and brought to Radio City as a permanent fixture. They turned out to be just the touch of live entertainment the place needed to set it apart from the city's other lavish movie houses. No ordinary chorus line, the selling point of the Rockettes was discipline and perfection, the ability to move as one dancer, with such precision that some audience members thought it was a trick accomplished with mirrors.

In subsequent seasons the Rockettes' fame grew as part of Radio City's annual Christmas show, where their routine as toy soldiers, complete with dominolike collapse at the end, became a signature part of the Christmas season.

Damon Runyon, reading posterity's mind the other day in the Mirror, *said he believed that twenty years from now the Rockettes would be a great metropolitan tradition. I've tried to believe that. The fact is we did meet a Rockette once. She came to a cocktail party at our house with a young man from the South with whom she had been to college. She was a plain, rather muscular girl who didn't drink or smoke, and her mind was wholly on her work. We tried multiplying her by a hundred in our head, but the effect, while prodigious, was still not stimulating.*

—Walcott Gibbs,
The *New Yorker*, October 14, 1939

Behold, the Christmas Movie!

Yes! Yes, I do! I like Christmas! I love Christmas!
—Reginald Owen as Ebenezer Scrooge
A Christmas Carol, 1938

Not to be outdone by New York, the West Coast was brewing up excitement of its own. It had recently made a big discovery—the blockbuster holiday movie.

Movies with Christmas themes had been around since the old two-reelers, but during the Thirties, Hollywood found that if you gave the movie an extra dash of something special—color, sentiment, big-name stars, lavish costumes, music—you'd be counting ticket sales far into the night. Laurel and Hardy departed from their usual fare to make *Babes in Toyland*, while Shirley Temple starred in no less than seven timed-for-the-holiday releases, including *Bright Eyes*, *The Littlest Rebel*, and *Heidi*.

Walt Disney scored hits with Santa-themed animated shorts early in the decade, but when word leaked out that he was working on a feature-length piece of animation, Hollywood turned skeptical. Cartoons, as everyone knew, were for children. No one, not even Disney, could charm people into sitting through an hour-and-a-half of such fare. Then there was the cost—$1,600,000, a staggering sum for any film at the time.

The skeptics, of course, were wrong. *Snow White and the Seven Dwarfs* premiered in

Los Angeles on December 21, 1937. Six days later, *Time* magazine put Disney on the cover—along with Bashful, Doc, Dopey, Grumpy, Happy, Sleepy, and Sneezy. Because movies opened in large cities first and worked their way down to smaller outposts in those days, most people couldn't see the film until the holidays were over. The wait and the word-of-mouth just heightened the excitement, and promises of being taken to *Snow White* were part of many youngsters' holiday haul. In the meantime, cards, coloring books, and just about anything with a *Snow White* theme were going like hotcakes. Hollywood learned an important lesson from Disney's Folly—never underestimate the desire of people to be entertained and delighted, especially at Christmas.

Town and Country

As late as 1939, electricity was still scarce in rural America, enjoyed by just one in four households. For folks who lived in the country, this made going to town all the more exciting. No matter how small the town was, it was sure to have brightly lit store windows, decorations, a dime store loaded with penny pleasures, and a movie theater.

For both country children and those in the city, school was another center of holiday activity. Weeks before the holidays, students began making gifts for friends and parents, decorating classrooms, and rehearsing for the annual program.

CHRISTMAS IN A ONE-ROOM SCHOOL

In 1935 or 1936, we had a wonderful rapport with the parents. We began having evening programs. The first one was Christmas. No electricity in the building. We had an organ you could either pump with your feet, or you could have one of the boys pump the handles.

Talking it over with some of the parents, we decided we would take a collection the night of the Christmas program. The money would be used to buy a piano and install electricity. The parents came and installed temporary electricity with long extension cords, all the way to the neighbor's barn, so we had lights for the Christmas program. The crowd was so large they stood outside on the porch shoulder to shoulder and at all the windows. Inside there was no room to get another one in to stand. We had a collection that evening of almost $225. In the Depression!

—Anna Neamand, teacher, Wimmer School,
Bucks County, Pennsylvania

We don't know how many students were in Anna Neamand's class, although a picture taken a few years later suggests she had as many as forty pupils. And we don't know how many parents, relatives, and well-wishers attended the program. We do know that it must have been a chilly evening for those standing at the windows—although no one seemed to complain—and we know that the sum raised, about $3,641 in today's dollars, was indeed an act of generosity in such hard times.

CENTRAL PARK AND BEYOND

There always seemed to be a lot of snow in Manhattan around the holidays. We didn't think about not having yards because there was Central Park, with Eagle Hill for sledding. There was ice skating on Central Park Lake and Irving Jaffe, a local favorite who'd won Olympic gold as a speed skater, gave lessons.

To me, Christmas was just one part of the New York winter. We didn't put up a tree, but set up a card table for our presents. I went to the Ethical Culture School, and there was a program each holiday season. When I was about six, I was chosen to be one of a group of children who would go onstage and say what they wanted for Christmas. When my moment came, I ran onto the stage and told the world, "I want a work bench."

I did get my little work bench, so it was a wonderful holiday for me. After Christmas, we went to the Château Frontenac in Quebec City, where the key attraction was the iced toboggan run. Later, we began to observe Chanukkah as well. But to me, the memories were all part of a chapter called Winters in New York.

—Robert Markel

A slice of joy will be my wish,
To fill your Merry Christmas dish.

Holiday parties of all sorts were popular during the 1930s, including parties to share with those in need. Civic organizations, church societies, and other groups frequently funded and organized Christmas Day dinners and children's parties. Railways offered discounted fares to those trying to join their families for the holidays. And many people, like Thomas Hughes and his wife, Florence of Scranton, Pennsylvania acted on their own. The young couple had endured hard times in 1935 and when things were going better for them in 1937, they decided to celebrate by inviting twenty-nine children to their home for Christmas Day. In addition to dinner with all the trimmings, each child received a bag of candy and nuts, an orange, an apple, and a gift—a doll for each girl and a red fire truck for each boy.

The focus of most parties, however, remained on family and friends. As Damon Keith's extremely wise father had noted back in 1929, simply being together in good health, without a link in the family chain being broken, was what made Christmas special.

Mike Reynolds, Chute Man

Undoubtedly one of the most impressive and eagerly awaited exits from any office party anywhere in the country was performed by Mike Reynolds, an employee of Macy's. Reynolds was the store's senior tunneler, one of those jobs little boys begin dreaming of the instant they hear about it. In those days, the store was equipped with a network of tubular chutes, each three feet high by two-and-a-half-feet wide on the inside. The chutes, distributed at various points around the store, began on the top floor and spiraled down to the main floor, with an access point on each level. Their purpose was to convey packages from various wrapping rooms down to the loading dock.

Of course, there were jams—especially at Christmas, when they could occur as often as two hundred times a day. Enter Reynolds, a veteran with twenty years' experience, who was more than up to the task of teaching the six tunnelers who worked under him the ins and outs of the business. Clad in overalls whose seat, like the surface of the tunnels, was waxed to reduce drag, Reynolds entered the troubled tunnel feet first and joined the tide of packages as they slithered along. When he reached the site of the jam he braked to a halt by wedging his feet against the wall. Then he untangled the mess and sailed on to the nearest exit point to await the next call to arms. According to the *New Yorker* reporter who interviewed him in 1939, the only time Reynolds was injured

on the job was once when a chair overtook him and gave him a bruising wallop. But just days earlier, he'd gone in search of a missing colleague and found him pinned between two large pieces of merchandise. The man was rescued without visible damage, and work continued.

As one might expect, Reynolds was an object of fascination, admiration, and not a little envy. He was in high demand at the annual post–shopping season employee banquet, held in the restaurant on the top floor. When it was time to call it a night, Reynolds' friends bid him farewell and watched as he dove into the nearest chute to spiral swiftly down the store's eight stories.

make it merry make it
MOJUD®

A word to every Santa from Portland to Atlanta!
To make the lady's Christmas *Merry*, give her
Mojud stockings. The stockings with Magic-Motion
. . extra "give" and spring-back in the knit.

Magic-Motion means longer wear, and more
fabulous fit from top to toe. Is your Christmas belle
tall, tiny or in-between? Ask for the Mojud stocking
length made especially for *her!*

stockings by
MOJUD

★ *Remember, there's lovely*
Christmas lingerie by Mojud, too

★ *At good stores everywhere.*
Or write Mojud Hosiery Co., Inc.,
385 Fifth Avenue, New York 16, N. Y.

War and Peace

For all intents and purposes, 1939 was the last Christmas of peace. A military draft was instigated in 1940, leaving many families separated over the holidays. The next year brought Pearl Harbor, and for the next four years, Christmas was a time of bittersweet longing. There were only a few questions that really mattered: *Is he safe? Is he coming home? When?* Peace had never been so much on people's minds, and when it came, the joy and splendor of Christmas burned brighter than ever.

I'll Be Home for Christmas

The tumult and dislocation of World War II was almost unimaginable by modern standards. Farm boys who'd never been over the state line found themselves on ships with populations bigger than the towns they'd grown up in. Women who'd never thought of working outside the home were putting rivets in B-17s—and liking it. Even so, Christmas brought a longing for the less-exciting times of old. No matter who you were or where you were or what you were doing, chances are that what you wanted most of all was simply to be home.

FROM BASTOGNE TO PENNSYLVANIA 6-5000

Worse than snow is freezing rain, and that is what they had at Bastogne, Belgium, for Christmas, 1944. Among the men enduring it was Captain Frank Lillyman, of the 101st Airborne Division. Months earlier, Lillyman had been the first man to touch down at Normandy, parachuting in at 00:15 on June 6.

On Christmas Day, Lillyman took his mind off the icy Belgian rain by jotting down some things he thought would make a perfect Christmas—to be back in the States, to be with his wife and young daughter, to sleep late and have breakfast in bed. As Lillyman pushed on across Germany with his division, he kept adding to his list. A week in New York's Hotel Pennsylvania sounded good, with a fresh flower for his wife every morning and a new toy for his daughter every afternoon. He also thought a phonograph with a selection of Strauss would be enjoyable, along with a telephone that blocked incoming calls, candlelit dinners *en suite*, and daily excursions for sight-seeing, theatergoing, and nightclubbing.

Lillyman saved for his dream. By the time the war ended and he was discharged, he had almost five hundred dollars. On his way home, he stopped in Manhattan, made his way to the Hotel Pennsylvania, and asked if it was enough to make his dream come true. The hotel management told him to put his money away, go home, get his wife and child, and return with them as soon as possible—the welcome home would be on them. For a week, just as he'd dreamed, Captain Lillyman had English tea in bed each morning and took all the hot showers he wanted. His wife had fresh flowers, his three-year-old daughter had toys and a nanny to attend her. The family dined on lobster Newburg and filet mignon and saw all the sights Manhattan had to offer. Bastogne seemed like a long way away.

The Christmas Look, Forties Style

Christmas during the war wasn't so much characterized by what you saw but by what you didn't see. In December, 1941 stores had few shoppers as the shock of Pearl Harbor redirected everyone's attention and cast a shadow over the nation. That year too, people were wary of an attack on the mainland. On the West Coast, the *San Francisco Chronicle* instructed citizens to turn off both houselights and Christmas lights when away from home, in case a blackout was declared.

In subsequent years, as America adjusted to being at war, people decorated and shopped again—so much so that whatever was in the windows or in the stores was often obscured by a tide of humanity. The war had created thousands of jobs, and pockets were flush for the first time in years. Shortages may have reduced the amount of things to buy, but people shopped anyway and celebrated Christmas as forcefully as ever.

After the war ended, though, the mood shifted, and it took a while for Christmas to get up and running again. There were still shortages of goods, and there was a cramped housing market that would take years to catch up with demand. Economic recession, though it never happened, was a real concern. Many chose to forgo a lavish Christmas in favor of saving their money or sending gifts of food and clothing to decimated Europe. Most families simply wanted to be together again. Old decorations and traditions would do just fine.

Tree and Trim

Christmas trees were one of the first shortages to surface during the war. The problem wasn't a scarcity of the trees themselves, but the lack of men to cut them. Tabletop trees, artificial trees, and bottlebrush trees took up some of the slack, and families with

men coming home on leave generally managed to have the real thing up and decorated, even if they had to pay more. Tree prices hit a high in 1942 and remained inflated until the troops were home again. By 1945, trees were plentiful again, and wholesaled for half of what they had three years earlier.

Before war broke out in Europe and interrupted international trade, most of America's Christmas ornaments had been imported from Germany or Japan. When Pearl Harbor was struck, many people left those ornaments packed away, while others destroyed them outright.

The war pushed America's fledgling ornament industry into high gear. Corning converted a machine designed to manufacture lightbulbs into one that could turn out two thousand glass Christmas balls a minute. Their biggest customer, Shiny Brite Ornaments, bought the blank glass balls, lacquered them, and added hand-painted details. When wartime shortages led to a shortage of metallic oxide pigment, Shiny Brite left the balls clear and added bands of color, to save on paint. Metal shortages led to another problem—a lack of caps and hooks for the ornaments. Some balls came with cardboard caps, while others came without caps or hooks of any kind, leaving those to the customer to supply. Homemade tree decorations were popular, as they had been during the Depression, and women's magazines usually carried directions and suggestions for creating a festive tree.

Another popular tree adornment was angel hair, which was scattered in white drifts on the branches. Made of spun glass, the stuff was literally irritating to work with, as the microscopic glass fibers worked their way into fingers and caused itchy discomfort.

The Household
MAGAZINE

December 1941 • 5 cents
ARTHUR CAPPER PUBLISHER

After the war, ornaments became full-color again, and Shiny Brite became known for it's trademark look—ornaments that had an exceptionally shiny, mirror-like quality. This was the result of using mercury glass, something the company had tried before the war but had to abandon for its duration. Also known as silvered glass, mercury glass contained neither silver nor mercury but was clear glass molded in a double layer, with a solution of silver nitrate poured between the walls to coat the glass on the inside. Mercury glass could be cast in a wide variety of shapes, it was lightweight, and its brilliant surface was just right for ornaments. The silver nitrate solution could be tinted every color imaginable, and further decoration could be added by painting the surface of the glass. Balls, tear drops, and icicles were all popular shapes, as were reflector balls.

Another popular post-war item was the angel tree topper. Made of hard plastic and often lit from within by a small bulb, the angel replaced the star as the finial of choice during the late 1940s and early 1950s. The most popular post-war innovation, however, was the bubbler light, the thin glass tube filled with colored liquid. It was always a magical moment when the tiny light concealed within the base heated the water enough to set it bubbling merrily.

Last Christmas I worried if my husband would come home from the office sober enough to trim the tree. This year I wonder if he'll come home from the Solomons—anytime.

— Young Navy wife, quoted in Time, December 28, 1942

Dressing Up the House

Candles in windows were a popular theme in the 1940s. You could see them on Christmas cards, but also in the windows of countless houses across the county. In addition to their coziness and cheer, the candles sent an unspoken wartime message as well—*We expect your safe return.* The candles weren't real, of course, but electric, made of the hard plastic that was being used in more and more items that had once been made of now-scarce metal. Many of the plastic candles also sported transparent plastic halos edged with glitter, and remained popular even after the war.

The new hard plastic was put to other holiday uses as well. There were Santas, sleighs, reindeer, and bells so hard and durable they actually seemed to chime when clanked together. Even cookie cutters were made of plastic instead of traditional tin, and came in holiday colors of red and, less often, green. After the war especially, there was a particular fad for tabletop churches. Molded of white or cream plastic, with a light bulb inside to shine from the windows, the churches came in varying degrees of elaborateness, from those with simple steeples and red roofs to styles as elaborate as Chartres,

Mr. S. Claus takes pleasure in announcing that—

bright new G-E CHRISTMAS TREE LAMPS are back again

Yes, bright new G-E Christmas Tree lamps will again be available this year . . . but in very limited quantities. However, the colorful, twinkling cheer that these little lamps bring this Victory Christmas, will—as usual—be unlimited.

The constant aim of G-E Lamp Research is to make G-E Lamps *Stay Brighter Longer*

G·E LAMPS
GENERAL ELECTRIC

trimmed with gilt and equipped with wind-up music boxes.

Another material used to brighten wartime homes was colored cellophane. Garlands of ruffled cellophane began to festoon mantels and doorways, as did cellophane molded into the shape of bells and bows. The most common decoration was the cellophane wreath. Hung on doors or in windows, in shades of red, coral, or green, plain or bearing an electric candle, these small circles of brightness were the stand-in of choice when real greenery was scarce.

Santa Sings Soprano

Another item in scant supply during the war was Santa himself as most "Santas" had been drafted by Uncle Sam. Competition for large, deep-throated men to ring bells and listen to children's wishes was fierce, igniting Santa wars among rival stores and putting a strain on bell-ringing charities. In 1939, the Volunteers of America had had fifteen Santas on the streets of Manhattan. The next year, a lone Santa was stationed in front of Gimbel's. He was no volunteer, either, but had taken the job on the promise of $2 a day and a $.25 lunch allowance. (Equivalent to $30 a day and $3.78 for lunch in today's dollars.) Rather than disappoint children, many department stores hired women to fill the void. Everyone made the best of it but, while millions of Rosies proved more than up to the task of riveting, there was something about a small woman in a big red suit that just seemed wrong.

Gifts and Greetings of the 1940s
To Send the Very Best

Christmas, 1944, won't be a merry one, honey . . . I can't be happy without you. But I shan't be too unhappy if I have some recent mail from you, and you are all right. As for you, dear, I hope all of your packages got there before Christmas; I hope you have a decent place to sleep, and decent food to eat, and don't be too lonely, dear. Remember that this is positively our first and last Christmas that we aren't going to be together. Think of all we have had, and just think of all we have to look forward to—years of happiness, and each year better than the last.

— Evelyn Alvery to her husband, Robert

Christmas greetings took on heightened meaning during the war. Evelyn Alvery's husband kept his wife's letter with him until his safe return at the end of the war. For him and millions of others, wartime cards were treasured as love tokens, charms against danger, and promissory notes for happiness to come. Cards for couples separated by the war bore sentimental messages like "Missing you" printed alongside sketches of a uniformed soldier and his girl strolling arm-in-arm into a sunlit future. Specialty cards were also made for mothers and sons, sisters and brothers, and friends of all sorts. Units stationed overseas frequently printed their own cards and stationery with cartoons of the unit mascots and messages like "Merry Christmas from the 42nd Bomb Group." Many were printed on parchment for air mail, and it was during this time that Hallmark introduced Hanukkah cards.

There was also a fair share of light-hearted offerings, and pop-up cards became a favorite new novelty. America's enemies—the leaders of the Axis—were often shown trussed up like Christmas turkeys and delivered as gifts to the Allies. Santa joined the war effort, and was frequently

... a size for every member of the family!

This Christmas—
**GIVE
WAR BONDS**

THE GENERAL TIRE & RUBBER COMPANY · AKRON, OHIO

shown dropping packages from bombers or donning helmet and goggles to command tanks.

Throughout the war, cards with patriotic themes were popular. Hometown porches flying flags were common, as were cartoons that depicted rows of tents with a wreath on each tent pole and soldiers decorating palm trees in red, white, and blue. Traditional themes with a sentimental twist were also common— bright poinsettias, stockings dangling from a mantel, snowy villages, sleigh rides, and churches with softly gleaming windows. Even after the war, cards retained their sentimental flavor, focusing on home, peace, and family reunited.

During the war, millions of people relocated, and many never returned to their hometowns. Christmas letters of the type we know today, with updates on the family's progress during the year, became increasingly common. This was the future that had been dreamed of for so long, and people were eager to share it.

SEASON'S GREETINGS, 1941

For many, the first Christmas of the war was a somber occasion. The first of Pearl Harbor's wounded were just arriving in San Francisco, and many families had already received notice of sons who were killed or wounded there. On Christmas Eve, President Roosevelt had been joined by Winston Churchill to address the nation. Even those who hadn't been personally touched by the events had few illusions about what lay ahead. At the Maloney home in Malden, Massachusetts, the mood was one of open grief—only days ago, they had been notified that their son, Joseph, had been one of the 2,400 killed in the December 7 attack. Though no one had an appetite, they went through the motions of Christmas dinner as usual. Midway through the meal, the doorbell rang. There, on the steps, stood a messenger waiting to deliver the most memorable Christmas card the family would ever know—a telegram from the War Department saying there had been an error. Private Maloney was very much alive.

Gifts of the Season

No one knows better than Macy's how wide awake America has suddenly become! In the past ten days, we've sold over a thousand globes, about eight hundred maps and hundreds more atlases! . . . all items are limited, the stock uncertain. Keep up with your soldiers, your sailors, your marines!

— Wartime ad

For the first time in years, the war put money in people's pockets to spend on Christmas gifts, and retailers who'd assumed holiday buying would be dampened for the duration were taken by surprise when 1942 rolled around. Many items were in short supply due to rationing and the fact that many manufacturers had devoted their production lines to war work. To the shoppers, this made not the slightest bit of difference. The stores became as crowded as the buses, trains, and subways, and customers lined up three- and four-deep to buy whatever was available.

Priority number one on everyone's list was the men and women away from home, especially those serving overseas. Lightweight gifts were recommended to conserve transport fuel, and one of the new inventions to achieve that goal is with us still—the paperback book. Expensive gifts were also discouraged, lest they be damaged or lost in transit, and the focus was on items that brought comfort or helped pass the time: warm socks, checkerboards, books, and magazines.

Food gifts were also common during the war. In 1942, Los Angeles candy stores were cleaned out well before Christmas, forcing retailers to impose a five-pound limit on customers who'd never in their lives bought more than a one-pound assortment. The minute the stores were resupplied, customers

SEARS, ROEBUCK AND CO., CHICAGO

waited in long lines to buy the full five pounds. Baked goods were favored by mothers, wives, and sweethearts who wanted to send something that tasted of home. Numerous articles gave rigorous and detailed packing instructions to preserve foods from the hazards of long transit—to little avail. Many food items arrived spoiled in spite of careful wrapping, for nothing could foil the mail ants, whose supply lines were the eighth wonder of the world. One serviceman scolded the *New Yorker* for printing overly optimistic directions for sending foodstuffs, assuring them they had no idea what elaborate tunnelings and massive depredations a squad of ants could create in a supposedly airtight fruitcake.

For those at home, gifts focused on the practical. Fuel rationing and colder-than-average winters made clothes such as sweaters, scarves, mittens, long underwear, and flannel pajamas a good gift bet. Household accessories such as towels, pillowcases, and kitchen gadgets were also popular, especially for war brides who'd married in a whirlwind and were still putting their households together. Since gas rationing kept people home more, gifts that could entertain were valued, too. Books and magazine subscriptions sold well, as did radios, and the board-game fad of the Thirties extended into the Forties.

At the outset, it looked as if children would suffer the most from wartime shortages. Traditional showstopper gifts like dolls and electric trains relied on materials no longer available, as did bicycles, tricycles, tin soldiers, basketballs, footballs, and just about anything else that required metal and rubber. Dolls could be molded from composite, a pulp made from sawdust and fiber. Though these weren't as durable as dolls made of rubber, thousands of little girls couldn't have cared less, and dolls remained the most requested toy for girls throughout the war—along with the usual assemblage of cradles, cribs, buggies, clothes, and trunks that went with them.

Boys who'd hoped for trains were encouraged to look ahead. Lionel made planning future train sets with Dad an activity in itself. In the meantime, "Militoys," introduced for the 1941 Christmas season, became a hit that lasted for the duration of the war. Tanks and transport vehicles, model kits of planes and ships—all accurate right down to the smallest insignia—let boys feel they were part of it all. Card games, board games, and action games with war-related themes flourished. In a card game called Thumbs Up, the winning combination wasn't a full house but three dots, a dash, and a V for Victory. In a well-liked board game, your game piece advanced if the spinner landed on "Aluminum," but set you back if it stopped on "Bottleneck" or "Fire in the Oil Fields." Target-practice games substituted enemy paratroopers and snipers for ducks and wild game. For older boys and teens, gifts that helped them track and keep up with battles and campaigns were in demand—globes, atlases, maps, radios, scrapbooks for news clippings, and bulletin boards with flagged pins for plotting troop movement—all became standard features of many adolescent bedrooms.

They are not wrapped as gifts (there was no time to wrap them) but you will find them under the lighted tree with the other presents. They are the extra gifts, the ones with the hard names . . . Atolls in the Sea. Assorted air strips, beachheads, supply dumps, rail junctions . . . Gifts in incredible profusion and all unwrapped, from old and new friends; gifts with a made-in-China label, gifts from Russians, Poles, British, French, presents from Eisenhower, deGaulle, Montgomery, Malinowsky . . . Gifts from engineers, rear gunners, private first class . . . there isn't time to look at them all. This is a Christmas you will never forget, people have been so generous.

— E. B. White
The *New Yorker*, December 23, 1944

Even before the war officially ended, gift giving began to change. Women became the focus of manufacturers who, anticipating the return of millions of men, predicted "a frank return to femininity." Ads assured Rosie the Riveter that "Froufrou becomes you." Sheer and sexy negligee sets, hats and scarves, and flattering dresses were all things women suddenly needed. Costume jewelry, bubble bath, dusting powder, and perfume were among the most popular gifts for women. Near the end of 1944, *Time* magazine noted that a huge, seventy-two-ounce bottle of Worth's *Dans la Nuit* was on offer for a staggering $1,000 ($12,048 in today's dollars). Despite the price, "it sold like patent medicine."

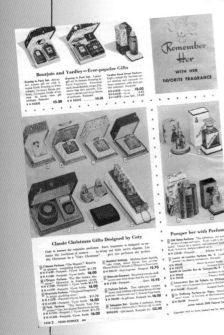

Men's postwar gifts were more practical, for all of them needed new civilian clothing. Four years of hard fighting had changed their measurements, and styles had changed as well. The majority of returnees were young men who hadn't established careers before they went overseas. They needed suits, shirts, overcoats, hats, briefcases—an entire wardrobe in which to fight the next war, making a living.

For children wanting toys, the end of the war brought no immediate relief. Shortages remained in effect, and factories took time to reconvert to domestic production. Chicago's largest store, Marshall Field's, had received only fifty-six tricycles to sell in the weeks before Christmas. In other large cities, new tricycles were going for two and three times their list prices, and used bicycles were selling on the black market for even more. Scooters, electric trains, and mechanical toys were unavailable at almost any price. Dolls were also scarce, due to a shortage of paint and stuffing as well as fabric for their clothes.

GIVE HER A LOVELY

Thayer

DOLL CARRIAGE

Things soon began to look up, however. In 1946, Lionel bought sixteen pages in *Liberty* magazine to run their entire Christmas catalogue. *Liberty*, recognizing a good thing, promptly added a cover featuring trains, and the issue sold thousands of extra copies. In some cities electric trains became a scarcity all over again, because every available set had been sold. The quality of toys also improved, returning to prewar standards, and new toys were once again invented. The Nina Ballerina doll was a huge hit in 1949, and Scrabble, Cootie, Clue, and Candy Land all debuted in the post-war years.

This week U.S. children had toys, candy and all the trimmings that traditionally go with Christmas. But it was a safe bet that no toy on Christmas Day aroused more ecstasy than a pair of new shoes given to a little boy in the U.S. zone of far-off Vienna. The little boy was an orphan. . . . The new shoes were issued to him, shortly before Christmas, by the American Red Cross. They and their radiant owner embodied, this year, the meaning of Christmas.

—*Time,* December 30, 1946

The Cost of Christmas: 1940s

Because of the inflation that took place during and after the war, the year is also given here, as well as the equivalent in today's dollars, listed in parentheses.

Christmas lights, per strand, 1941: $1.39–$1.98 ($20.15–$28.70)

Christmas tree, five feet tall, 1941: $.75 ($11.35)

Pepsi-Cola, 1941: $.23 for six twelve-ounce bottles ($2.75)

Kraft Philadelphia Brand cream cheese, three-ounce package, 1945: $.11 ($1.35)

Hamburger, per pound, 1943: $.25 ($3.10)

Ham, per pound, 1948: $.57 ($5.05)

Beef pot roast, per pound, 1949: $.43 ($3.85)

Stuffed Spanish olives, two-ounce jar, 1947: $.43 ($4.10)

Baby carriage, 1947: $27.00–$35.00 ($257.10–$333.35)

Teen's holiday dress, 1946: $14.95 ($162.50)

Boy's snowsuit, 1946: $10.00–$13.95 ($108.70–$151.65)

Women's nylon stockings, per pair, 1945: $.95–$1.60 ($11.35–$19.05)

Women's "Plenty of Nothing" black lace panties, 1945: $25.00 ($297.60)

Men's Van Heusen shirts, 1942: $2.25 ($29.60)

Movie camera, Ciné-Kodak Eight, 1940: $97.50 ($1,477.30)

Record player, automatic, 1947: $25.95 ($247.10)

Silvertone portable radio, 1948: $24.95 ($220.80)

RCA Victor TV, 1949: $199.95 ($1,785.30)

Movie ticket, 1942: $.35–$.50 ($4.65–$6.60)

Tricycle, 1945: $47.50 ($565.50)

Globe, 1941: $2.79 ($40.45)

Ray gun that shoots sparks of light, 1944: $.44 ($5.30)

Flexible Flyer sled, 1947: $8.95 ($82.25)

Plastic dollhouse, complete with TV set and plastic furniture, 1948: $8.95 ($79.25)

J. C. Higgins girl's bicycle, 1949: $49.50–$56.50 ($442.00–$504.50)

Lionel electric train set, 1947: $22.50–$75.00 ($214.30–$714.30)

Buttons and Bows

The war put an end to the opulent papers and coordinated wrappings that had become popular in the Twenties and the Thirties. Like cards and decorations, wrapping paper and ribbon weren't rationed outright, because the War Office believed preserving customary holiday traditions was a matter of national morale. However, paper shortages made both paper and ribbon expensive and hard to come by, and the paper that was manufactured was so thin it tore easily. Despite this, wrapping paper sales actually increased during the war. After the war, paper became plentiful again but remained thin by today's standards. What it lacked in substance, however, it made up for in brightness and cheer—intense reds and greens, repeating patterns of candy canes, poinsettias and holly, snowmen cavorting across drifts of pale blue snow, all proclaimed the joy of the season.

Have Yourself a Merry Little Christmas

After the first shock of being at war had passed, Americans recovered their equilibrium and adjusted to life on a war footing. Young men who had been tucked away in colleges or living in isolated small towns until Pearl Harbor, found themselves flung together by the tide of war. Shipyards, bases, and training camps, always meant boom times for whatever town was nearby. Many young women left home as well, to serve with the Red Cross or join various branches of the military. People bound overseas wanted to enjoy themselves as much as possible, and those headed home on leave felt exactly the same way.

Subtly and not so subtly, the government encouraged Americans to keep their spirits up by enjoying things that could still be enjoyed. And there was much to enjoy, especially in the cities. Movies, music, shows, roller rinks and ice rinks, dances sponsored by innumerable volunteer groups, cabarets and nightclubs and dance bands and ballrooms—for those lucky enough to be stateside, there were plenty of distractions. If, that is, you could get in. Nightclubs were so crowded that comedian Jimmy

Durante had a running joke about losing a shirt button and trying to retrieve it before an overeager waiter could unfurl a tablecloth and seat four customers at it.

In New York, the Shuberts donated use of their 44th Street Theater to the American Theater Wing for their Stage Door Canteen, a place where servicemen in transit could relax, enjoy some music, and have a bite to eat. Top-flight entertainers like Ethel Merman and Ethel Waters performed free of charge, waitresses worked on a volunteer basis, and coffee, sandwiches, and desserts were donated by local caterers and restaurants. Any serviceman passing through town was welcome—not only Americans but British, Canadians, Australians, Dutch, Chinese, French, and Russians.

Also important in keeping up morale was the United Service Organization. The USO had come on the scene in 1940 to alleviate the boredom of military life for men who'd been drafted. Their Camp Shows were so popular that in 1941 the government asked them to be responsible for entertaining troops at home and abroad. They had no trouble convincing top-billed singers, comedians, film stars, dancers, and even whole Broadway shows, to volunteer their time and talents.

Despite the fact that many actors were themselves serving overseas, movies boomed during the war. In the 1930s, Hollywood had learned that movies and Christmas were a natural match. In the 1940s, it learned that movies, Christmas, and wartime nostalgia was audience catnip.

Movies of the 1940s echoed the themes of war, separation, and reunion in a peaceful, and idyllic world. Frolics like *Christmas in July*, *Christmas in Connecticut*, and *Holiday Inn* were counterbalanced with bittersweet entries like *Since You Went Away*, *I'll Be Seeing You*, *Meet Me in St. Louis*, and *The Bells of St. Mary's*. The postwar years produced two of the best-loved Christmas classics of all time—*It's a Wonderful Life* and *Miracle on 34th Street*—both of which perfectly captured the optimism of an America that was young and hopeful once more.

PUGET SOUND, 1944

I worked as a civilian secretary for the Navy during the war so I could be with my husband at bases he was stationed at. Lots of young couples did that, there was always a crowd of us around. One year, when we were at Puget Sound, two other typists and I went to see *Since You Went Away*, with Claudette Colbert. It was around Christmastime, and I felt so sorry for those two other girls. The Battle of the Bulge was going on, and had been for several days. We knew it was a terrible battle, with heavy losses. They both knew their husbands were there, but hadn't had any news. They could barely sit through the movie, they were so fretful. It must have been an awful Christmas for them. I never found out what happened to their husbands. Either they got transferred or we did. There was a lot of moving around in those days.

— Elsa Lindquist Waggoner

Even more important than movies was the popular music of the era. Songs did double duty during the war. First, they were entertaining in themselves, and soldiers could listen to their favorite songs on Armed Forces Radio. More than that, music helped bridge the distance between home and away. A girl in Portland, Oregon, listening to "In the Mood" could remember dancing to it with her fiancé and know that her fiancé, far away, would have the same memory when the song was played.

Songs of the decade were rich with melody and sentiment. Like movies of the era, they focused on themes of love, parting, home, and the longing to be reunited. Christmas songs were no exception, and the decade spawned a generation of modern carols that have since become classics. By far the most popular was "White Christmas," which debuted in 1942 and quickly became the most requested song in the history of Armed Forces Radio. It was followed by "I'll Be Home for Christmas" (1943), "Have Yourself a Merry Little Christmas" (1944), "Let It Snow" (1945), and "The Christmas Song" (1946).

Postwar Christmas music became distinctly more light-hearted, with offerings like "It's a Marshmallow World" and "Mele Kalikimaka." And for anyone who hadn't noticed there was a baby boom on, tunes like "All I Want for Christmas is My Two Front Teeth," "Here Comes Santa Claus," and "Rudolph the Red-Nosed Reindeer" drove the point home.

Coming Home

Eventually, of course, the war ended. Over the weeks and months that followed, servicemen and others who'd been overseas for the duration made their way home. For some, home was a permanent destination. For others, it was a temporary way station from which to reassess and regroup. And for still others, the millions of children born since 1940, life went on much as it always had.

POSTWAR PEACE NEAR COUNCIL BLUFFS

December 25 on the farm started like all other days, even for me, the youngest of thirteen. Our farmhouse had just three bedrooms, one for the older boys, one for the girls, and one for us six youngest boys. My parents slept on a hide-a-bed in the living room. All of us got up around 5:00, and I was soon on my way to help with the milking.

Christmas started when we came in from chores. There, on the table, we'd see that Santa had come and left gifts for each of us on our plates. They weren't big gifts— small items, candies and nuts and oranges, and new clothing like a shirt or a pair of overalls—but it was always exciting. Later, we had our regular family gifts. We kids always drew names, and part of the fun, besides getting your own present, was seeing who had drawn whose name, and who had given what to whom.

There was the big traditional dinner, too. One turkey wasn't enough, so my mother usually made at least two. These, all the vegetables and potatoes and gravy and dessert—everything was made on a wood-burning stove that we kept fueled with wood and corncobs. My folks had gotten electricity the year I was born, but we wouldn't have indoor plumbing until the early 1950s, so when it was time to do dishes, you had to fill a kettle with water from a pump at the sink, then heat it on the stove. Start to finish, dinner was a big production.

In later years, when my older brothers got married, they came back with their families for Christmas. Then we'd have at least forty people, and my mother was disappointed if we didn't have fifty or sixty. One year, when we had the money, all of us went together and got her a forty-inch-wide gas stove with a double oven.

Those Christmases didn't have the bells and whistles that Christmases do now. No electronic games, no after-Christmas sales, no winter vacations to ski or lie on a beach. But I feel sorry for anyone who's never tramped through the cold, fading blue of an Iowa morning and wondered what Santa left on his plate.

—Keith Casson

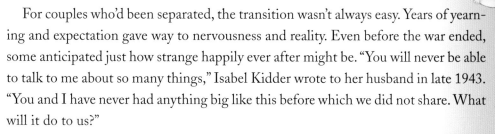

For couples who'd been separated, the transition wasn't always easy. Years of yearning and expectation gave way to nervousness and reality. Even before the war ended, some anticipated just how strange happily ever after might be. "You will never be able to talk to me about so many things," Isabel Kidder wrote to her husband in late 1943. "You and I have never had anything big like this before which we did not share. What will it do to us?"

Aside from the psychological adjustments, there were practical ones as well. Inflation was high, and many feared a return of recession and unemployment. Many men who'd had jobs before the war found they had them no more, and young men who'd enlisted out of high school and in the middle of college had the challenge of starting careers in a world completely unlike the one they'd left. One of the biggest challenges was housing—there wasn't any. Not enough, anyway, to accommodate all the new families that had formed over the past few years.

America had lost its small-town feeling and become a bigger, richer, and slightly less familiar place. Even Christmas didn't seem quite the same at first, with family and friends scattered across the country, and some gone forever. But gradually, people found their way. They rebuilt relationships, found new jobs and new places to live, and celebrated Christmas for all they were worth.

It's a tree-triming party and each guest can play Santa Claus by hanging his share of tinsel and bright balls on the tree. Set the time for six-thirty, just when the night begins to turn dark, and have the scene set with the bare Christmas tree in a stand, already set up before the guests arrive. Round the tree are heaped mysterious "presents," all the same shape and size and wrapped in the same gay silver paper with big blue bows . . . well, you've guessed it! It's the party supper, all wrapped up and pretty enough to eat!

—Ladies' Home Journal, December 1949

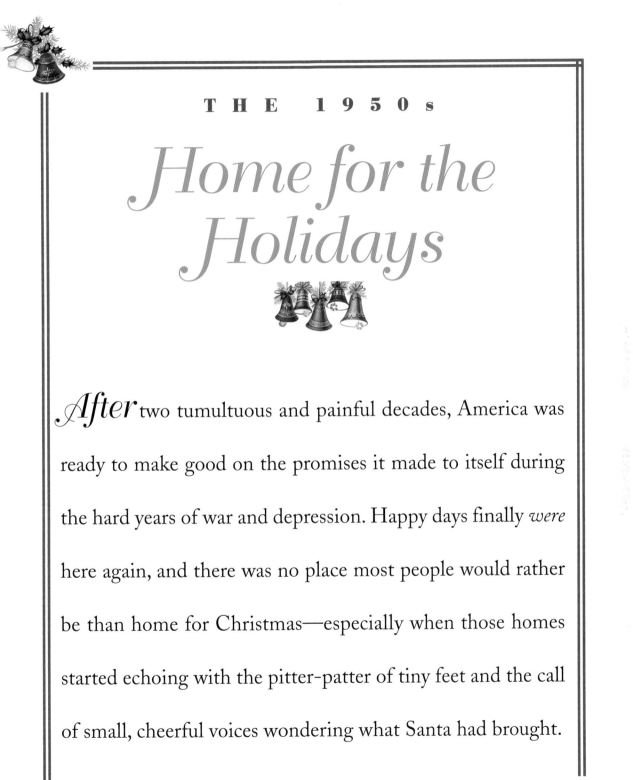

Home for the Holidays

After two tumultuous and painful decades, America was ready to make good on the promises it made to itself during the hard years of war and depression. Happy days finally *were* here again, and there was no place most people would rather be than home for Christmas—especially when those homes started echoing with the pitter-patter of tiny feet and the call of small, cheerful voices wondering what Santa had brought.

a real ROY ROGERS Christmas!

ONLY REAL
ROY ROGERS western
clothes, toys and school
supplies are branded with
the Double R Bar label. So look
for it when you're Christmas shopping.
You pay no premium for this
assurance of top quality.

Holly and High Anxiety

The decade renowned for peace and prosperity didn't start on the plush note it's remembered for, nor was it ever completely anxiety free. The atomic flash that ended World War II cast a shadow of uncertainty over the future. There was a new thing called the Cold War to worry about, which soon spawned a war of its own. Many men who'd thought they'd never spend another Christmas overseas found themselves recalled for active duty, along with younger men who'd barely been in their teens when the last war ended.

IF I EVER GET HOME, I'LL NEVER BE THIS COLD AGAIN

Christmas, 1951, was my first Christmas to be away from family and friends. I was beginning to feel sorry for myself. Like many servicemen, I was in Seoul, Korea, wishing I were in Mississippi. Mail call for the 15th Radio Squadron, Mobile, was a few days before Christmas. I can hear my name—"REDDEN"—being called by the sergeant. Two small packages had arrived and I was thrilled. One was a can of Maxwell House coffee that I shared with two buddies. The other was a tin of Hebrew cookies from Mother. It was my favorite treat for Christmas, and Mother's secret family recipe! Mothers never forget.

On Christmas Eve, we had a real treat. Thirty children from a nearby Christian orphanage came dressed in Korean-style clothes and sang Christmas carols in English for the 15th R.S.M. There were tables set up so we could have the Korean children intermingle with us at each table.

What a night to remember! When the children left, there were tears flowing down the cheeks of each soldier.

The next day, Christmas Day, men who were off duty could go to the Bob Hope USO show in Seoul. Eligible to take in the show were those who could crowd into the only six-by-six-foot truck that would run. The theater building was one of the very few buildings left standing after the destruction of the city of Seoul. We arrived about 3:00 p.m. and the show started at 7:00 p.m. The temperature was zero degrees Fahrenheit, and it seemed that thousands of troops were standing very close together, trying to keep warm, waiting for the doors to open. I do not remember everyone from the show, but I do remember Walter Pidgeon, Debbie Reynolds, Carlin Carpenter, and Les Brown and his Band of Renown. And, of course, the headliner was Bob Hope. After a few Bob Hope jokes, I almost forgot where I was.

—Walter Redden

The Christmas Look, Fifties Style

Both the old war and the Cold War subtly shaped the look of Christmas throughout the 1950s, but not as much as two other staples of the decade—children and an economy that was nothing short of swell. Financial columnist Sylvia Porter was the first to connect the dots and give the new generation its identity. "Take the 3,548,000 babies born in 1950," she wrote in 1951. "Bundle them into a batch, bounce them all over the bountiful land that is America. What do you get? Boom. The biggest, boomiest boom ever known in history."

In the early years of the decade, even retailers were caught by surprise. Merchants worried that people were buying too much, especially when post-Christmas sales surged. "Why are you buying so much, New York?" Macy's asked in a full page ad. Concluding that the spending spree was spurred by fear of shortages, the store admonished the public to curb its appetite.

Buy nothing out of fear. Buy only what you need or can use. But don't buy one extra thing because of "what might happen." There are goods enough to satisfy our needs. But there can never be goods enough to satisfy our fears.

—Macy's ad, January 1951

The buying didn't abate, the shortages never developed, and wages continued to rise. In 1956, *Time* magazine ran a wry article about the dilemma of churches, which could not locate poor to donate to at Christmastime. For the past three years, churches in Mayfield, Kentucky, had resorted to newspaper ads to track down those in need. Another church, in Nashville, Tennessee, had vastly liberalized its definition of *needy*—and was still unable to dispense all of its gift baskets. The Fifties were, and would remain, a tsunami of plenty. Never in the history of the world had so many ornaments, lights, gifts, toys, trees, and decorations been sold—so many that, by the end of the decade, Christmas looked entirely different than it had at the start.

Nothing in the world could induce us to give up our old-fashioned Christmas tree in the living room, but we are toying with the idea of utilizing extra ones elsewhere for decorative effect. Aunt Elsie has told us about a friend of hers who keeps a tree in the hall, on which she hangs all of her Christmas cards. Last year, one of our neighbors used a dining table centerpiece, which would be especially effective in a home where there are youngsters: a tiny fat spruce hung with candy canes.

—Elisa Bialk, *Household*, December 1950

Tree and Trim

In 1950, a Gallup poll discovered that 73 percent of households that put up a tree put up a real one. It was a high-water mark that would never be equaled again. Artificial trees had always been available, but for the most part they were "instead-of" trees—small tabletop trees made of feathers or larger models made of brush-style bristles to use when the real thing was in short supply. In the late Fifties, all that changed. An artificial aluminum tree, dubbed the Silver Pine by one of its manufacturers, burst on the scene like a blond bombshell. The aluminum tree was the Marilyn Monroe of Christmas trees—glamorous, alluring, and flaunting its artificial look like a tiara from Tiffany's. Some featured branches with realistically spiked needles; others had delicate, tinsel-like needles; still others were covered with what seemed to be long, flirty eyelashes of curled metal. Although they came in a variety of colors—including gold, red, blue, green, pink, and blends of silver and other colors—by far the most popular

For the Brightest Christmas Ever!

G-E

Be sure to get Christmas Tree Lights by

GENERAL ⊕ ELECTRIC

color was plain silver. Lights could not be used on the trees due to the danger of shock, so the finishing touch was a rotating color wheel that sat on the floor in front of a floodlight, bathing the tree in a changing rainbow of shades.

With the creation of the suburbs, people had more room, indoors and out, and began to put up more than one tree. In addition to the living room, there was often a den or family room to be decorated. Outside there was a yard with trees that begged for lights. Multiple trees were no longer just for the White House.

Ornaments of the Fifties were similar in style and shape to those of the Forties. Colored balls and reflector balls of shiny mercury glass were still popular, especially at the beginning of the decade, as were clear, colored glass balls painted with thin bands of color or stenciled design. In the early part of the decade, the colors remained the deep reds, greens, and golds that had prevailed in the Forties, but as the decade wore on, the colors became the cool tones of the atomic age. Silver and platinum were favored over gold, and intense turquoise, ice white, lime, and even raspberry replaced traditional red and green.

Of course, lights had to offer something new as well. Strands of multicolor lights became less common in the second half of the decade, replaced by single color lights so the tree could be decorated according to a precise color scheme. In keeping with the cool colors of the era, GE introduced lighted ice bulbs, spheres coated with glassy flakes that, when lit, sparkled like real ice crystals. Flashing lights were also introduced at this time, along with the light that would become the signature light of the coming years—the tiny "midget" or "fairy" light.

Inside, Outside, and All through the House

Much was expected of the housewife of 1950s. Unlike housewives of the past, odds were that she'd been to college, worked during the war, worked before her children were born—and possibly all three. Freed from the drudgery of housework by a legion of modern appliances, she was expected to train her formidable talents not on keeping house but on creating it. As one magazine of the era put it, her house was to be "an ornament to the neighborhood"—especially at Christmas.

Earlier generations had bought decorations for the house ready-made, but crepe paper swags and honeycomb bells would have looked woefully out of place in the four bedroom suburban ranch rambler. Instead of ready-made decoration, the woman of the Fifties was expected to create her own wreaths, mantelscapes, and centerpieces, all tailored to match the decor of her home. There are no one or two standard decorations from the 1950s, but hordes of them: handmade angels, driftwood painted white and dusted with silver glitter, large mirrors wrapped with red satin bows, vine baskets piled high with pinecones, and modernistic gilded deer leaping across dining room tables. It was a formidable responsibility, and it's amazing how many women rose to the occasion.

Outside the house was Dad's province. During the 1950s, more than five million acres of brush, potato fields, sandlots, and prairie were transformed into yards. Few suburbs had anything like a Main Street or a town square to decorate, so homeowners took matters into their own hands. It began with a few lights around the picture window or on the evergreen in the side yard that seemed to be crying out for them. Then the smart aleck across the street showed off his athletic abilities by climbing a ladder and outlining his entire roof in lights, and the neighbor two houses down made a plywood Santa that all the kids were going nuts over. Manufacturers did their bit by producing giant

plastic candles and almost-life-size carolers. Before you knew it, local papers began running features about the best-lit extravaganzas, people drove by to look, and friendly competitions broke out all over the place to see who would become the Light King of Blue Heaven Drive.

The secret of successful entertaining lies in providing your guests not only with good food and attractive surroundings, but also with an atmosphere of warmth and charm.

—Blanche Halle, *The Art of Entertaining*, 1952

Gifts and Greetings of the 1950s
Good Tidings We Bring

Sometime after the war the world got much younger, and greetings of the era reflected the new mood. Cards of the early Fifties used the same bright colors as those of the late forties, but the subject matter was lighthearted and joyful. Poinsettias were replaced by candy canes, frolicking snowmen, and exceptionally jolly Santas. Mrs. Claus appeared more often, celebrating a family theme, and the young were everywhere. Children, puppies, and Bambi-like fawns abounded, and even husbands and wives were portrayed as supernaturally youthful. The style itself was bright and exuberant, often creating the sense of a richly animated Disney cartoon.

In keeping with the new mood, humor played a more important role than it had in the past. Several card companies, including Hallmark, created lines of less formal cards that delivered a punch line, either by way of the art or the written message. Santa was often shown racing along in a car with sweeping tail fins or relaxing in front of a huge TV. Even nuclear jitters were soothed with a dose of humor. As the Cold War grew more intense and the space race ignited, Santa and his sleigh were shown dodging everything from Sputnik to Soviet missiles—usually above a message that read *Peace on Earth, Goodwill toward Men*.

The family Christmas letter also continued to flourish, now with a new innovation—the photo card, sometimes of the whole family but more often of the children posed on Santa's lap or hanging stockings by a fireplace.

Like everything else, cards developed a streamlined, contemporary look as the decade progressed. The four-fold cards of the past became less common, and the simpler, single-fold card became the standard. Hallmark's Studio line introduced a tall, narrow card that became known as the Slim Jim. Near the end of the decade, cards began to switch away from childlike subjects and the cartoon style and colors of the early years to reflect the modernist perspective. Stylized nature scenes, often involving pale pastel forests, silvered deer, and glittering banks of pearlized snow, became extremely popular.

In the 1950s, almost everyone sent cards. Special address books and card file boxes with seasonal decorations were marketed to the busy card-sender to keep track of the dozens and dozens of family members, hometown friends, war buddies, bosses, workmates, bridge club members, and neighbors who must not be forgotten. Card sending reached such a fevered pitch that in 1956 Army Chief of Staff Maxwell Taylor issued an edict to the nearly twenty thousand people working at the Pentagon: If you want to say *Merry Christmas* to your co-workers, do it in person, because the Pentagon's postmen could no longer cover the miles it took to deliver the masses of cards through the labyrinthine distances of the building. The national tide hit an all-time high in 1958. Never before or since had so many cards been mailed by and to so many Americans.

Dear Santa Claus,
Please bring me a cowgirl suit. I want to wear it to school and have fun.

Your friend,
Louise Marie Gross
Juan, Kentucky, December 1952

Gifts of the Season

For most people, gift giving in the Fifties was more lavish than ever before. Neiman Marcus set the pace in 1951 when it started featuring outrageously luxurious His and Hers gifts in its Christmas catalogue. On offer that year were a set of matching vicuña coats ($695 each—$5,696 in today's dollars) and a pair of Swiss watches ($90 and $145—$737 and $1,189 today, respectively). Subsequent years would bring such gifts as Black Angus steaks on the hoof, ermine bathrobes, Chinese junks, and matching airplanes.

I get backaches from waiting on these people. If business was any better, I'd be in the hospital.

—Cheerful Dallas retailer, *Time*,
December 20, 1954

The catalogue was a publicity stunt, of course, but it reflected America's rising affluence. Retailers who'd initially been suspicious of the high rate of spending accepted it as the new normal. Accommodating shoppers wasn't easy. Most stores closed at 6:00 or 7:00 P.M., and laws prevented commerce on Sundays. Then, in 1951, a newly opened shopping center in suburban Boston tried something radical. They decided to stay open until 9:00 P.M. on Wednesday, Thursday, and Friday nights. Commuters could now come home from work, eat dinner, then shop at their leisure. The move was such a success that Shopper's World decided to extend their hours indefinitely, and other retailers began to follow suit.

People had always wanted a "big Christmas" for their children, but now adults joined the gift-a-palooza. The Spartan, homemade gifts of the past all but disappeared, replaced by the kind of gifts people wouldn't buy for themselves. Multiple gifts became commonplace—husbands and wives gave each other personal items, but there was often a larger family gift as well. Most often the gift was something for the house, such as new furniture, a TV set, a dishwasher, wall-to-wall carpeting, a freezer, or hi-fi with AM/FM radio. America had become a cornucopia of new and enticing consumer goods, and there was often enough money to buy them.

Just in time for Christmas

ANOTHER GREAT PHILCO FIRST...
<u>FULL</u> REMOTE CONTROL TELEVISION!

FROM ACROSS THE ROOM, YOU CAN

1. Turn the Set On
2. Select Your Channel
3. Adjust Volume
4. Adjust Fine Tuning
5. Adjust Picture Contrast
6. Change Stations
7. Turn the Set Off

● **COMPLETE REMOTE CONTROL AND BALANCED BEAM TELEVISION** in this luxurious Philco Model 2176. Great 215 sq. in. true-focus picture on a 20 inch gray filter-face rectangular tube...with Philco's superlative No-Glare Optical System, Electronic Built-in Aerial, and sensational Custom-Duplex Chassis. Powerful, golden-toned AM-FM radio and Philco phonograph that plays *all* records automatically. The absolute ultimate in a combination!

NOW a giant 20 inch <u>true-focus</u> picture that you can control from across the room

ANOTHER unprecedented triumph in Philco engineering! Never before in any set has full and complete remote control been possible. But now Philco enables you to control your set completely—turn it on or off, adjust the picture—without rising from your easy chair!

Only Philco has it! And only Philco gives you Balanced Beam Television which *balances* the electron *beam* that "paints" the picture on the tube . . . locks it in positive focus over the entire picture area. Now you can enjoy thrillingly sharp, clear pictures . . . entirely free of blur or smear . . . the first true-focus picture in television history.

But these are only two of Philco's great advantages. The new 1951 Philcos offer you the sensational Philco Custom-Duplex Chassis which means vastly increased sensitivity, performance, and picture quality with remarkable freedom from "ghosts" and "snow," and other interference.

The new Philcos also have the famous Philco Electronic Built-in Aerial that outperforms all others by as much as 3 to 1.

Compare Philco point by point with any other set! Compare for picture quality . . . tone . . . design . . . value. Prove to yourself that Philco Balanced Beam Television tops them all!

● **HUGE 20 INCH TELEVISION** in distinguished mahogany console. 215 sq. in. *true-focus* picture, 20 inch gray rectangular tube. Model 2134, $429.95. Complete range of new Philco 1951 table models, consoles and combinations, 97 to 215 sq. in. pictures, 12½″ to 20″ tubes, in distinguished mahogany, walnut or blond decorator type cabinets from $169.95 to $750.00*.

TUNE IN! *Philco Television Playhouse, Sunday evenings, NBC-TV Network . . . Don McNeill's TV Club, Wednesday evenings, ABC-TV Network.*

AND BEST OF ALL, A **PHILCO**

*Tax and Warranty extra on all models. *Prices slightly higher in South and West. Prices subject to change.*

Even the smaller personal gifts were more luxurious. Clothes weren't given because they were sorely needed but because they were fun. Husbands collected golf clubs, outdoor grills, and fishing boats and motors. Wives found themselves in possession of expensive perfume, good jewelry, and fur-trimmed coats.

Undoubtedly Santa's happiest thought is this big, beautiful Westinghouse Refrigerator. It's the family larder ... Styled for 1952 ... built for years of carefree enjoyment. And it's the perfect gift that means good health and better living for all. You can be SURE ... if it's Westinghouse

—Christmas ad, 1951

For children, the holiday was even brighter. Many couples had put their family plans on hold because of the war. Others, who'd grown up in the shadow of the Depression, waited until they had money in the bank and a manageable mortgage. Born into an unusally secure world, children of the 1950s might as well have arrived wearing T-shirts that said *I'm Here for the Party*.

Manufacturers were quick to mine the crop of new customers—and their parents. All-grown-up little boys who'd never gotten their own electric trains now got them for their sons. By 1955, Lionel was selling $33 million worth of goods a year. In competing for the toy-buying market, manufacturers had a powerful new ally—television. Children's shows gave toy makers an entire universe of heroes and heroines to spin product from. No longer could a marionette be just a marionette—it had to be the Howdy Doody marionette. Not just any toy six-shooter would do, it had to be the Hopalong Cassidy six shooter. When Dale Evans starred in a Saturday western with husband, Roy Rogers, girls caught horse fever and began asking for cowgirl outfits, boots, and horses named Buttermilk.

Television also helped market toys that had nothing to do with the shows themselves. When quirky, innocuous Mr. Potato Head became the first to buy TV ad time, sales jumped to $4 million in just one year. In the past, news of toys had spread from child to child by word of mouth, and parents could steer Junior away from temptations like Christmas catalogues and toy windows. Television allowed toy makers to show the toy directly to the children it had been designed for. The result, more often than not, was a mania among the five-to-twelve-year old set for licensed characters and name-brand toys. The competiton was fierce and the desire of toy makers like Marx, Ideal, Hasbro, Kenner, and others to produce the toy everyone wanted led to some of the most unique and creative toys in the history of childhood.

As Seen on TV: Must-Have Toys of the 1950s

1950 Buzzy Bee pull toy, Hopalong Cassidy lunch box, Nina Ballerina doll, Tiny Tears doll, Silly Putty

1951 Ginny doll, View-Master

1952 Colorforms, Mr. Potato Head

1953 Gumby, Winky Dink Magic TV Screen, Winnie Walker doll

1954 Mouseketeer ears, Robert the Robot, Davy Crockett coonskin cap, Matchbox cars

1955 Wooly Willy, Cissy doll

1956 Ant farms, Miss Revlon doll, Play-Doh, Yahtzee

1957 Frisbee, Wheel-Lo, Jill doll

1958 Hula Hoop, Toni doll, Pitiful Pearl doll, Prehistoric Times play set

1959 Little People, Visible Man

The Christmas season in my childhood of the 1950s is filled with memories of my maternal grandparents. They lived on the edge of Roger Williams Park on the Providence-Cranston, Rhode Island line where the winter meant sledding and skating in the park. My father worked for his father-in-law, which meant that after school was finished, we spent all of the holidays at my grandparents' house. My grandmother had a lot of friends, and the women would have a Christmas tea and open house and sell the handmade dolls, decorations, and baked goods to people who streamed in and out. I watched them from my special spot under the grand piano.

The house was decorated and the tree was bought by the time we arrived, and the house was filled with the smell of freshly baked cookies and gingerbread. On Christmas Eve, the grownups would give each other "joke" presents in a family tradition where they got to pick on the person whose name they drew at Thanksgiving with a gift and a poem. They thought I was asleep but I hid on the landing and listened to them laugh good-naturedly at each funny gift and at each other.

Gifts from Santa were not wrapped but placed under the tree for me to play with while the grownups opened gifts to each other. I enjoyed arranging my gifts under the tree and having my picture taken with them. One Christmas I was very sick with the measles and the doctor made a house call. My grandfather kept me amused by reading from a tiny book called *Little Squirrel's Christmas*, making mistakes on purpose so I could correct him. As it happened, that was his last Christmas with us. After he was gone, my grandmother moved to a large apartment. We carried on with Christmas as before, but it was never quite the same as the wonderful holidays spent in their beautiful English Tudor house, when all the important people in my world were there.

—Midge Frazel

The doll I am touching has a knob on the top of its head that spins the face to ones of different expressions. I can remember the scratchy wool bathrobe and my feet are hot in the slippers.

The Cost of Christmas: 1950s

Inflation was generally mild during the 1950s and what there was was more than made up for by rising wages. *Contemporary equivalents in today's dollars are listed in parentheses and rounded to the nearest nickel.*

Artificial tree with fireproofed boughs: $5.95 ($43.45)

Sirloin steak, per pound: $.89 ($7.10)

Lamb chops, per pound: $.75 ($5.90)

Whitman's Sampler, one-pound box: $2.25 ($7.90)

Nestlé Chocolate Chip Morsels, six-ounce bag: $.19 ($1.50)

Canada Dry ginger ale, two twenty-eight-ounce bottles: $.45 ($3.60)

Men's calfskin shoes: $9.98–$17.98 ($79.25–$142.70)

Men's dress shirt: $2.89 ($21.25)

Women's wool coat, with mink trim: $79.00–$139.00 ($627.00–$1,103.00)

Women's dress shoes: $7.99–$18.95 ($60.55–$143.60)

Westinghouse refrigerator: $319.00 and up ($2,614.75 and up)

Gas range, thirty-six inches: $98.00 ($720.60)

RCA twenty-one-inch black-and-white TV: $99.00 ($798.40)

Sears Craftsman 2.5-horsepower lawnmower: $66.65–$89.85 ($490.10–$660.65)

Bar-B-Q Brazier grill, with legs: $7.80–$11.98 ($57.35–$88.10)

8mm movie camera and light bar: $55.00 ($436.50)

8mm movie projector and screen: $75.00 ($585.95)

Mickey Mouse lunch box: $.88 ($7.10)

Children's cowboy boots: $4.95–$7.95 ($39.90–$64.10)

Girls' tap shoes: $3.00 ($26.55)

Ginny doll, in underwear: $1.98 ($16.30)

Outfit for Ginny doll: $1.00–$2.98 ($8.20–$24.40)

Cootie game: $2.00 ($15.90)

Deluxe's Senior Chemistry Set: $11.25 ($101.80)

Robert the Robot: $5.98 ($47.50)

Satellite launcher with rotating radar tracking station: $4.98 ($37.70)

Visible Man: $4.98 ($36.35)

ORIGINAL SLINKY $1.00

SLINKY SOLDIERS $2.00

SLINKY SEAL $1.00

SLINKY HANDCAR $2.00

SLINKY
SPIRAL $1.00

SLINKY DOG $2.00

Insist on

Slinky® Toys

AT YOUR NEAREST TOY COUNTER

Packages of the Fifties, like the homes of the era, were meant to reflect the individuality, artistry, and care of the giver. While gift wrap sets were still sold, components from which to create your own unique packages were also offered. Silver- and gold-foiled paper, and heavy cellophane in brilliant greens, reds, and turquoises were sold as basic ingredients, to be matched with trimmings of all sorts. There was a special passion for tie-ons— little embellishments such as sprigs of artificial holly, papier-mâché Santa faces, and tiny snowmen made of pipe cleaners that were meant to be added to bows and gift tags. And if regular ribbon wasn't creative enough, 3M made a line of opaque tape in shades of red, white, green, or gold, decorated with holiday patterns like bells, holly leaves, and bows. One of the most curious offerings were thin transparent plastic straws that came in holiday colors and were meant to be snipped into short bundles, tied at the center, and fanned into pom-poms.

Let the Good Times Roll

When people begin to complain that Christmas has become too big, too commercial, too noisy and bright, and so over-the-top that we're losing the meaning of the whole thing, you can pretty much conclude that just the opposite is taking place. At least that was the case in the Fifties. With little else to worry about, people began to find fault with the nation's biggest holiday. Santa Lands and department store windows were more glorious than ever, and charmed a new generation of children with fairy-tale tableaux and visions of magic, yet so vocal were those who protested the absence of religion that in 1952 Dayton's department store in Minneapolis was goaded into partitioning the store into a secular side and a religious one. The religious side of the store, with a beautiful nativity scene, was kept scrupulously free of the Santas, sleighs, and trees that adorned the rest of the store.

As for music—Bah, humbug! "Who is listening?" *Time* magazine demanded in 1957:

> The music boom sometimes seems less a cultural awakening than a mammoth assault of indiscriminate sounds on a public that no longer has any place to hide. Amateur psychologists say that the U.S. is becoming afraid of silence. In this holiday season, the musical voice of Christmas carries to vacationers paddling beneath the surface of Miami pools (via underwater loudspeakers), to women in slenderizing salons, to celebrators in non-slenderizing saloons. In Philadelphia, worshipers can drop by the Arch Street Methodist Church and adjust a selector to the hymn of their choice. From the highest building in Salt Lake City, Christmas carols boom across the Salt Lake Valley.

The article went on to quote an "irate" woman who, while not wanting to "sound like Scrooge," complained that her fellow citizens were forcing her to go without sleep until December 26. Besides store windows, Santas, and music, the holiday season was too long, children were being spoiled with too many gifts, there were too many movies and secular distractions, and to top it all off, instead of staying home people were taking to the traffic-snarled roads like tumbleweeds in a dust storm.

The outrage fell on deaf ears, and the noise, clamor, and fun continued. Movies like *A Christmas Carol* and *White Christmas* drew huge audiences. Those wishing for a silent night had to plug their ears as a bumper crop of new songs—including "Frosty the Snowman," "Silver Bells," "Sleigh Ride," "It's Beginning to Look a Lot Like Christmas" and "The Little Drummer Boy"—filled the air. Tunes with a pop twist, such as "Santa Baby" and "Jingle Bell Rock" must have seemed a particular affront, while kiddy tunes like "Frosty the Snowman," "I Saw Mommy Kissing Santa Claus," and "The Chipmunk Song" must have had the staid and straight-laced reaching for their aspirin bottles.

The complainers had missed the point. A holiday losing its grip isn't celebrated too long or sung too loudly. Church attendance was high throughout the decade, and Christmas programs and pageants were part of many people's holiday tradition.

Other entertainments may have seemed distressingly modern, but most of them revolved around spending time with children, friends, and family. Much of the music and a good share of the holiday movie and television fare of the 1950s was unusually family oriented. Even the nuclear defense monitoring system got in the spirit and

The Year-Round Gift of Greater Viewing Comfort

deployed their resources to track Santa on his rounds and deliver hourly bulletins on his progress.

In 1954, Balanchine's full-length revival of *The Nutcracker*, the most child-friendly ballet imaginable, became a national sensation. As for the thousands who clogged arterial highways and boarded crowded trains, it was more often to be with far away family members than to escape a home that bored them with its lack of distractions.

Despite the endless array of things to do in the 1950s, and the funds with which to do them, most people celebrated modestly. Just one year after lamenting the noise of Christmas, *Time* magazine noted that the Christmas office party—the bacchanalia that had once worried wives and tested husbands—was definitely on its way out. Peace, prosperity, the move to the suburbs, and the birth of millions of children had changed much in America. When it came right down to it, home was where most people wanted to be.

MY CHRISTMAS, 1954

Each year, in the weeks before Christmas, my cousins and I rehearsed a play to perform on Christmas Eve in the solarium of my aunt's house. The solarium didn't have a door but a wide proscenium arch that made it a perfect stage. One aunt directed our rehearsals while another worked as costume and wardrobe mistress. My mother designed and typed programs, which she ran off on the ditto machine at her office. Sometimes we put on O. Henry-like tales of sentiment and sacrifice, other years we did the Christmas story. As the youngest of the cousins, I seldom had a speaking part, but I didn't care. My older cousins were glamorous to me and I was thrilled to be the manger lamb or the waif-like—and usually mute—orphan girl.

December 24 came with the excitement of Christmas and a Broadway opening rolled into one. People dressed up, as people did in the Fifties. The women wore glitter in their hair and Christmas corsages, the men wore cufflinks. That year, my grandmother made the women gauzy red hostess aprons with ruffles and hand-painted white poinsettias. There was even a small apron for me. It's hard to imagine now that people would get so dressed up just to sit in a living room, open presents, and watch children put on a play, but that's what they did. My father and uncle panned the crowd with their Super 8 movie cameras, light bars drenching us with such blinding wattage we really did feel like movie stars.

My usually frugal parents threw caution to the winds that year and bought me a very expensive Madame Alexander doll. My dad made a doll trunk, which Santa left under the tree. It was painted with bright red lacquer and had brass corners and a latch with a tiny padlock. Inside, there was a drawer with a small glass knob, hooks, a rod with hangers for doll clothes, and the same wallpaper I had in my bedroom. It was magical to me that Santa knew what kind of wallpaper I had.

I still have the doll and the trunk, and the memory of that Christmas, when we were all so young and sparkling.

—Susan Waggoner

The Holly Jolly Christmas

It was the decade when everything changed—or so they said. The Cold War pushed nerves to the breaking point, youth ran wild, and just about everything else went into a blender and came out as confetti. A Beatles Christmas album? Who saw that coming? Not to mention the fact that chartreuse trees with purple decorations were suddenly the height of chic. Yet beneath the funky gift wrap and DayGlo tinsel, Christmas was much the same as it had always been. Thank goodness.

Christmas with the President

Dear President Kennedy,

Please stop the Russians from bombing the North Pole because they will kill Santa Claus.

Michelle Rochon, age 8
Marine City, Michigan, October 1961

Dear Michelle,

You must not worry about Santa Claus. I talked with him yesterday and he is fine. He will be making his rounds this Christmas.

President Kennedy

Seldom had there been such a visual passing of the torch as there was from President Eisenhower to President Kennedy. Though both had served in World War II, there was a generation's worth of distance between them, and Kennedy's youthful vibrance struck a chord with the nation. Looking to the White House, Americans saw a family much like their own, with young children, a wife who strove to make a beautiful home, a husband who'd come home from the war determined to make the most of peaceful good times, and a close-knit extended family. People felt a personal connection to the Kennedys they had not felt for other White House families, and were intensely interested in how and where they spent the holidays, especially when it came to Christmas.

The whole family gathered for one of those Kennedy living room games, not charades but kind of like a variety show. Some of the family got up and did skits, or jokes. I played some Chopin, Jackie read a poem, a serious one I remember, certainly not Ogden Nash, probably Edna St. Vincent Millay. Jack then decided that he was going to sing! And he said, "Joansie, please accompany me on the piano." I was terrified. He didn't have a great singing voice and he kept changing key. I managed to follow his voice and keep changing keys on the piano. But Jackie knew what I was doing. She came up afterwards to me, "Joan, you are a terrific musician because you made Jack sound great."

—Joan Kennedy, former wife of Ted Kennedy,
The Kennedy White House, Carl Sferrazza Anthony

The Christmas Look, Sixties Style

Festive, Fanciful Decorations

The spare, ice-cool look that came into style with the Cold War modernism of the late 1950s continued into the 1960s. Part of its popularity was undoubtedly due to the fact that millions of modern homes had just been built, and the style was a flattering fit for the houses. The look also fit the national mood. America in the Sixties—especially the early 1960s—was entranced by visions of the future. The Cold War had spun off an unexpected source of entertainment, the space race, and as America caught up with and eventually overtook the Russians, the future seemed brighter and brighter. Glimpses of an uncluttered, streamlined future were everywhere, and people loved what they saw. Ironically, it was a look that aged quickly. From mid-decade on, America began to envision the future in a different way, a way that, while still different from the past, exchanged the streamlined look for new complexities of form and color.

Tree and Trim

Real trees had been falling out of favor since the 1950s, replaced by artificial greens and one of the most popular trees of all time, the aluminum tree with its rotating color wheel. A new kind of tree was also gaining in popularity—the flocked tree. Home flocking kits had debuted in the 1940s but the process was messy, required a vacuum cleaner and never caught on as nationwide trend. In the 1960s, professionally flocked trees became widely available. Better looking than the do-it-yourself variety, professionally flocked trees could be used for more than one season. All the homeowner had to do was choose the color and take it home. Moreover, the choice of colors was lavish—white and powder blue were initial offerings, but soon purple, gold, pink, lime green, bright blue, red, and even black became available.

The other tree trend of the era was started by Jacqueline Kennedy in 1961, when she created the first themed tree in White House history. Based on *The Nutcracker*, the tree was adorned with miniature wooden nutcrackers, toy soldiers, tiny wrapped packages, and candy canes.

It wasn't long until themed trees became a fad across America. The old hash of varicolored lights, balls, and garlands

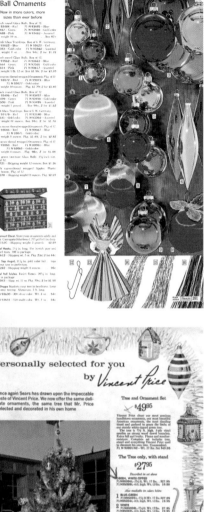

would no longer do, and those striving for elegance were urged to create a new theme each season.

The Kennedy-style tree became a lasting White House tradition. Lady Bird Johnson chose an Early American theme for her tree, which featured gingerbread cookies, popcorn, and fruit. Pat Nixon's tree featured ornaments representing the fifty states.

Ironically, the glistening, blatantly artificial aluminum tree that had been so popular early in the decade was felled by an unlikely foe: an animated Christmas special. *A Charlie Brown Christmas*, first aired in December of 1965, was the beginning of the end for the aluminum tree. When Charlie Brown rescued the little tree that was homely but real and found in it the true meaning of Christmas, children began to clamor for a real tree of their own, or at least an artificial tree that looked real. It was a request most parents found hard to refuse, and within a few years the aluminum tree vanished from the scene.

Although the flocked tree remained, it too suffered a decline, and was never again as popular as it was in the mid-1960s.

As pop art flourished in the second half of the decade, ornaments became more innovative, incorporating bold color combinations and nontraditional materials. Balls wrapped in shiny rayon thread were especially popular, and came in a wide variety of colors.

And, despite qualms about artificiality, Americans simply could not resist plastic. Hard plastic had been used in decorations since the Forties, but in the Sixties soft plastic reigned supreme.

The new plastic was easier to shape and to color. It could be poured into molds or rolled thin as paper. It could be clear, translucent, opaque, or a gradient of all three. It could even be flocked, and accepted paint and glue in a way hard plastic did not, making it easier to trim.

Best of all, soft plastic was inexpensive, and parts could be mass-produced and fitted together with other parts and materials to create items that looked ornate and complicated. Tiny plastic angels and Santas appeared on trees, along with plastic garlands. There were also plastic balls, whose manufacturers promised a "glass-like" look. When lead tinsel was outlawed, plastic tinsel—both metallic and multicolored—stepped in to fill the gap. One of the most common ornaments of the time was a clear plastic ball, teardrop, or lozenge-shape "crystal" with a sprig of plastic holly, a tiny bell, or a snowman visible inside.

Indoors and Out

In the Sixties, as in the Fifties, homemakers were expected to deck the halls in a way that reflected creativity and individualism. Now, however, the homemaker had help. Manufacturers countered fears of living in an era of depersonalization with a free-market solution: endless novelty. Never had so many doodads been offered to so many buyers at such low prices. The enterprising homeowner could pave the lawn, cover the house, and fill every inch of interior space with holiday knickknacks and still produce something entirely different from anything the neighbors would come up with. It was the Great Age of Novelty, laden with pinecone candle rings, candy dishes that chimed "Jolly Old St. Nicholas," and fireplace matchboxes with Santa's face on them.

Outside, lightweight shatterproof Santas could be spotted on chimneys, along with sleighs led by a full complement of reindeer. Plastic holly and evergreen garlands wrapped porches and railings in seasonal good cheer, and plastic poinsettias could weather any storm. Plastic fruit created a fad for Della Robbia decorations outdoors and in, and garlands or wreaths of greenery studded with apples, grapes, lemons, oranges, and pears lent the sophistication of the sculptor for whom the look was named.

It's a Marshmallow World

Mail-order houses boomed in the Sixties, and Kmart, Wal-Mart, and Target all opened their doors in time for Christmas, 1962. The result was a cornucopia of novelties meant to delight, amuse, and not be taken too seriously. Below, a sampler:

• "Deck the Halls" doorknob cover in red and green felt, with jingling bells.

Stocking Stuffers

• Santa-faced felt switch-plate cover, complete with Santa cap.
• Set of four Santa mugs whose handles spell *N-O-E-L*.
• Santa-faced ashtray.

• A chandelier of metallic-foil discs to reflect a rainbow of holiday hues.
• Fireplace-size four-foot electric candles with candy cane stripes and dripping wax "flames."
• Electrically lit star tree topper promising to make you feel "as though the blazing Star of Bethlehem Were Passing in Its Orbit at Your Home."
• Tabletop musical church with colorful stained glass windows, playing "Silent Night."
• Donder and Blitzen salt and pepper shakers.
• For dad, shorts with his name, Santa, and holiday bells painted by hand.
• For mom, jingle-bell panties with a real bell and hand-painted candy canes.
• For the girls, matching candy-striped flannelette housecoats.
• Press-on window scenes featuring snowmen and reindeer.

Slippers for Holiday wear. Gold color plastic

• The Three Wise Men in heavy weatherproof plastic, to be mounted on the side of the house.
• For the yard, 3-D carolers in full color, singing "O Come, All Ye Faithful."
• Battery-lit Santa doorknocker emblazoned with the family name.
• Five-by-six-foot banner for the garage door wishing passers-by a Merry Christmas.

Gifts and Greetings of the 1960s
Peace on Earth

Cards of the early 1960s were similar to those of the late 1950s, favoring woods and snow scenes and embellished with details like foil embossing, flocking, and glitter. Humorous cards that mirrored current events were also still popular—in the Sixties, Santa dodged Russian satellites and went to the moon.

By mid-decade, psychedelic colors and pop art style entered the mix, along with flower children and hippies flashing the peace sign. Though the hippies were a subject of humor, peace wasn't—as the Vietnam War became less and less popular, more and more cards featured the dove of peace and wished *Peace on Earth and Goodwill toward Men* rather than the traditional *Season's Greetings*. Another sign of the changing times was that for the first time, Hallmark began creating cards for the African-American community.

One card line of the late Sixties seemed doomed to fail. In the midst of moon landings, peace protests, and bold poster art, American Greetings licensed Holly Hobbie, a storybook character whose calico bonnet, homespun pinafore, and long stockings hearkened back to simpler days. Although she seemed completely out of sync with the times, she was an enormous hit and was featured not only on cards but on Christmas plates and towels, ornaments, and table decorations well into the Seventies.

When Donald and Jean Meyers of Charlotte, North Carolina, were married in the early 1940s, they hoped to have a large family with at least a dozen children. After having two girls and adopting two boys, they decided that four children was all fate meant to give them. Then Donald read of a car accident that had taken place in Minnesota shortly after Christmas of 1961, leaving nine children without a mother or father. He told the story to his wife, who voiced exactly the thoughts he'd been thinking: "If those children were put in the world together, they should stay together."

Christmas week of 1962 found the Meyers family, along with several reporters, gathered at the Charlotte airport. The occasion was a festive one—they were there to welcome their nine newly adopted children. "We aren't being wonderful," Jean Meyers told a reporter from *Time* magazine. "We need children. We want these children. We are going to have a lot of fun."

With that, the family of fifteen set off for home, to begin preparations for Christmas.

Gifts of the Season

Here, in its entirety, is the list of what an eight-year-old girl friend of ours wants for Christmas: 1. A Bible 2. A deck of cards.

—The *New Yorker*, December 3, 1960

In a December 21, 1962 article cheerfully entitled "The Blight before Christmas," *Time* magazine reporters consulted psychotherapists, concerned members of the community (including a Canadian mother who claimed Santa's arrival by helicopter "confused her children hopelessly and made them miserable"), and their own gut instincts to conclude that Christmas was no time to rejoice. Rather, it triggered bouts of alcoholism, marital infidelity, unbridled eating, and family quarrels. It depressed those who'd had unhappy childhoods because they had no pleasant memories, and depressed those with happy memories because the present didn't measure up.

No element of the season, however, was as fraught with emotional hazard as gift-giving. Husbands who could not afford everything the family wanted passed bad checks and felt "inadequate in the male role." Parents "agonized" over disappointing their children while adult children found that choosing a gift for Mother was "a traumatic experience."

Then there was the wealthy relative whose gifts could not be equaled, the marginal friends you had better buy something for in case they bought something for you, and the greedy brigade of newspaper boys, mailmen, doormen, and others who expected an annual tip. And when the revelry was over? "The ghost of Christmas past comes [back] in the form of another monthly payment at the bank." Bah, humbug!

Fortunately, no one paid the slightest attention to *Time*'s experts, and rushed headlong for all the trauma, agony, indebtedness, and disappointment Christmas had to offer. For most, the financial good times of the 1950s continued to roll right through the 1960s, so much so that by 1966 *Time* ceased railing against gifts and focused on helping people give *the right* gift. "What, in short, does one give in the society that has everything?" The answer, in no uncertain terms, was *everything*. In a society that already has everything, you give more of the same, leavened with whatever new gags and gadgets can be found.

Overheard in a Peter Cooper Village playground, tall lady to son: "Money, money, money, money! Is that why we got you the Book of Knowledge *for Christmas?"*

—The *New Yorker*, January 13, 1962

Families continued to buy large gifts that could be enjoyed by everyone in the household—black-and-white TVs were replaced with color sets, second cars appeared in driveways, boats and campers and trips to Disneyland became possible for more families than ever before.

Though *Time* continued to trumpet the virtues of an agonizing search for the one perfect gift, those on the receiving end had no such qualms. Gift cards did not yet exist, but wish lists were no longer just for children. Many department stores set up "stag shops," where wives put their wish lists on file. All a husband need do was show up, request his wife's list, and decide which of the gifts to buy. And while he was at the shop, the store had him fill out a card of his own.

Although it took the surprise out of Christmas, that wasn't necessarily a bad thing. A Seattle woman said she had no qualms about requesting a beige mink pillbox hat, because the year she hadn't filled out a card she'd received a garbage disposal for the

kitchen sink. According to *Time*, "the blight of depersonalization" was even worse in the young, who were increasingly asking for cold cash because, as one Boston teen explained, "If they buy it, it's always wrong."

Perhaps because people expected to receive most of the things they truly wanted, novelty gifts took on an unusual importance in the Sixties. Many people gave them in addition to serious, big-ticket presents, and they seemed worth every penny—when present-opening time came, all you could really do with Waterford crystal or a new table saw was ooh and aah, but everyone could enjoy Dad walking around in his official *Apollo 11* mission cap saying, "Tranquility Base here. *The Eagle* has landed." Other popular novelty gifts of the era included troll dolls, mood rings, lava lamps, love beads, peace symbols, tie-dye T-shirts, fallout shelter handbooks, alcohol flavored lollipops, and slogan buttons that asked questions like *Is there intelligent life on earth?* and *Nixon's the one—is Humphrey one, too?*

share the fun...
FAMILY STYLE
launch your holiday dream with an Evinrude for Christmas

EVINRUDE *quiet outboard motors*

Children also continued to benefit from the decade's prosperity, and toy makers of the Sixties outdid even their Fifties predecessors in creating fun, fascinating and, above all, name-branded playthings that became classics.

Although Barbie, the *über* doll of the century, had debuted in 1959, mothers were initially resistant to her. There was a general consensus that no doll should look that good in a sweater, but by 1960 Barbie was the doll every little girl wanted—and usually got.

As opposite from a teen fashion model as could be was another classic toy for girls, Kenner's Easy-Bake Oven. From its debut in 1964 right through the Seventies and beyond, the Easy-Bake stayed at the top of the toy heap, and though its look and color options changed over the years, its charm never did.

For boys, the space race, with its emphasis on science and technology, led to the creation of classics like wind-up robots, three stage rockets that poured real smoke, and kits to build your own transistor radios and elementary computers. Other popular toys for boys mirrored those popular with girls. Boys weren't interested in Barbie, but in 1964 they got their first major action figure—G.I. Joe. Like Barbie, Joe had an impressive array of accessories to wish for, only his weren't party dresses and Dream Houses but Navy SEAL gear, helicopters, jeeps, and tanks.

And just as the Easy-Bake Oven proved an instant hit with girls, so did Mattel's Thingmaker capture the imagination of boys. In retrospect, one wonders why it hadn't been invented sooner. Give boys a toy that allows them to manufacture an endless supply of bugs, spiders, worms, and centipedes; requires the use of something called Plastigoo; and is slightly dangerous to boot (many floor coverings still bear scars from over-heated goo), and there will be an all-out stampede to the toy counter.

As Seen on TV in Living Color: Must-Have Toys of the 1960s

1960	Chatty Cathy doll, Etch-A-Sketch
1961	Mr. Machine
1962	Tammy doll
1963	Mouse Trap Game, Give-a-Show Projector, Troll Doll
1964	Easy-Bake Oven, Thingmaker, Mighty Tonka dump truck, G.I. Joe
1965	Operation, Rock 'Em Sock 'Em Robots
1966	*Lost in Space* Robot, Liddle Kiddles, Spirograph, Twister
1967	Frosty Sno-Man Sno-Cone machine
1968	Hot Wheels

The Cost of Christmas: 1960s

Like the Fifties, the Sixties was a decade of relative economic ease. Inflation was not excessive and, for most people, rising wages more than compensated for any increase in price. *As always, contemporary equivalents in today's dollars are listed in parentheses and rounded to the nearest nickel.*

Wrapping paper, twenty-seven-inch roll: $.94 ($6.20)

Fifty-light strand of miniature lights: $3.29 ($22.70)

Aluminum tree, six feet tall: $11.29 ($77.90)

Lawn Santa, lit from within, forty-two inches tall: $16.50 ($108.55)

Candy canes, package of six: $.25 ($1.80)

Land o' Lakes butter, per pound: $.49 ($3.30)

Porterhouse steak, per pound: $.89 ($6.20)

Turkey, whole, per pound: $.43 ($3.10)

Ice cream, half gallon: $.59 ($4.10)

Men's lambswool pullover: $8.99–$11.99 ($60.75–$81.00)

Men's Arrow shirt: $4.00 ($27.00)

Women's suede coat: $88.90–$120.00 ($600.70–$810.80)

Women's dress shoes: $5.90–$19.97 ($39.90–$134.95)

G.E. dishwasher: $149.95 ($1,071.00)

RCA color TV: $358.88 ($2,424.90)

Transistor radio: $8.49 ($58.95)

Ping-Pong table, five feet by nine feet: $19.95 ($142.50)

Chatty Cathy: $10.98 ($78.40)

Bendable Barbie: $2.79 ($18.40)

Easy-Bake Oven, with mixes: $8.99 ($59.15)

Play-Doh, five two-ounce cans: $.49 ($3.10)

View-Master viewer with three Batman reels: $2.78 ($18.30)

Lost in Space Robot: $7.95 ($52.30)

Cape Canaveral Missile Base set, with phonograph of launch countdowns: $7.98 ($57.40)

Tiger guitar, with amplifier: $19.88 ($130.80)

Wrap Warp

When you're sophisticated, you can wrap a gift in a newspaper. But if you haven't arrived yet, you keep up with the Joneses.

—Sol Weiner, president, Chicago Printed String, 1960

In the 1960s, gift wrap and ribbon exploded with variety. In addition to traditional designs, an entire universe of new colors and novelty designs came into the market. More than ever before, wrappings played off of the culture around them. Mimicking an early Sixties passion for bleeding Madras shirts, paper was offered that gradually faded from one color to the next. Peter Max–inspired paper wished everyone *Joy* and *Noel* in curving pink, marigold, purple, orange, and green letters that seemed to expand while you looked at them. *PEACE* and *LOVE* were repeated in poster-size letters on paper

whose neon shades of chartreuse, aqua, and red made you long to close your eyes. Purple and hot pink bells on a gold background had much the same effect.

So big had the gift wrap business become that companies began to cater to markets within the market. According to Sol Weiner, president, Chicago Printed String, Texans and those on the West Coast preferred elaborate wrappings. Floridians liked palm trees on their paper and, like other Southerners, had little use for paper that featured snow scenes and snowmen. For reasons Weiner could not figure out, New Englanders refused to buy anything with birds on it.

Ribbons, too, offered more variety than ever. Satin ribbon and ready-made stick-on bows largely replaced old-style curling ribbon. Companies also offered "package garters," elasticized bands that fit almost any size package, and came with a bow or gift tag affixed. Near the end of the decade, fat, fluffy twists of yarn became popular for tying up packages, and came in bright colors like acid green, bright red, purple, and electric blue.

Christmas was usually celebrated with just our immediate family, so it tended to be a quiet holiday. Because of this, some of my favorite memories are of the family traditions we established during the holiday season, like driving around on Christmas Eve between dinner and present opening to look at houses decorated for the holidays, and working a jigsaw together.

One of the things I looked forward to most was going to downtown Minneapolis on a Sunday morning to look at the store window decorations. We looked at all the windows, but Dayton's were especially dazzling—dozens of windows filled with winter and holiday scenes. The best ones would have animated characters like elves

working in Santa's workshop or ice skating on the North Pole. The stores weren't even promoting merchandise in the windows. They were just scenes that made you smile and made you excited to think that Christmas was coming.

After walking the stretch of what is now Nicollet Mall, we'd go to breakfast at the Forum Cafeteria. This seemed like another fantasy world to me—pushing a tray along the "endless" track, picking whatever you wanted to eat. Items you'd never consider eating at home looked very tempting set out for selection. After eating, we'd often go to a large drugstore, where my sister and I could purchase something. Since stores weren't open on Sundays back then, the drugstore was about the only place that was open. I really can't remember what I'd pick out, maybe a new coloring book or crayons or paper dolls. My sister remembers that she once got a small flocked deer that our mother set on a piece of driftwood to make a little snow scene. It didn't really matter what we got, because the real presents were still to come.

Little did I know that this particular year, 1960, I would get my favorite gift ever, a beauty parlor doll. This was the ultimate package—a doll that could actually bend at the knees, a swivel salon chair and all the plastic accessories: lipstick, shampoos, curlers, there was even an old-fashioned hood-style hair dryer on a stand. I had never seen anything like it before, and to this day, no one I've ever met had a doll like that. Things are so different now, where kids all want the same item—usually what's advertised heavily.

—Peggy Nylin

The Fun Frontier

I like Christmas day. I go here and there. I eat cake, gingerbread and other foods. I have many good times. One Christmas we went to five houses. First we went to Great-Grandmother Gray's for breakfast and a Christmas tree. Then we went into our living room to open our presents. We went to our Grandmother Gray's. We went to Grandmother Stewart's for Christmas dinner and more presents and a Christmas tree. Then we went to Great-Grandmother Helm's for supper. Then we came home. Mother threw up.

—Anonymous eight-year-old boy,
quoted in the *New Yorker*, December 1, 1962

Despite the havoc that played out on the national stage in the 1960s, people who lived through the decade remember having a good deal of fun. People still visited family and got together with friends, but there were more things to do outside the home than ever before. Although malls were springing up across America, people still went downtown to see the sights. If anything, downtown stores went to even more elaborate lengths to dazzle customers—even if they didn't buy anything that day, they would remember the store fondly and, quite likely, shop the branch store at the local mall.

In their December 10, 1965 issue, the often-curmudgeonly *Time* magazine opened an article on city spectacles with salutary awe. "Nineveh saw nothing like it," the piece read. "Imperial Rome would have been abashed, and Solomon, in all his glory, could not have afforded it. It is America's great Christmas festival." The article went on to note that Rich's department store in Atlanta routinely spent so much money on decorations it no longer kept track, but estimated the price at $150,000 (approximately $1 million in today's dollars). Its tree-lighting ceremony, held Thanksgiving night, positioned four choirs on each of the four floors of a glass-enclosed bridge over a pedestrian mall outside the store. As each floor came alive with lights, its chorus burst into song, the grand finale being the illumination of a sixty-five-foot white pine as all the choruses and crowd sang "Silent Night." For those who missed the tree-lighting, two pink monorails with pig faces for fronts ferried children around the tree in a continuous loop.

Time went on to note San Francisco's tradition of decorating Union Square's sixteen-foot-tall yew trees with hundreds of colored lights, and Fort Worth's skyline lit with bright geometric patterns. Even once-Puritan Boston had finally given in and begun decorating Boston Common with thousands of white, orange, and blue lights laced across the bare branches of the park's elms and spruce trees brought in for the occasion. During the day, visitors could enjoy a Nativity scene featuring seventy-five identical white sheep with one black sheep leading the flock.

Liddle Kiddles Klub

Kiddle Kottage

Liddle Kiddles are as small as your child's hand. And as big as her imagination.

Tiny dolls are cute, but they're nothing new. Except for our nine Liddle Kiddles.
Here's what's new about them: each tiny doll has a personality all its own. Each one has arms and legs that really bend, and hair that little girls can brush and comb. Each one comes with a Liddle Kiddles story book. And finally, each Liddle Kiddle comes with a toy that really works. (For example, Liddle Diddle has her own crib. And the sides really do slide up and down.)
All of this is why the Liddle Kiddles *are* something new. They're part of a whole tiny world. A child's world of imagination. We feel that's a pretty nice thing.

The Liddle Kiddles Klub (left) is another of our new kind of doll houses. It's big enough for all the Liddle Kiddles. We also have a Kiddle Kottage (above), just the right size for one Liddle Kiddle.

124

As for New York, no city could hold a candle to it: "At dusk, virtually every square foot of street frontage in midtown Manhattan comes alive with winking wreaths, sparkling and mechanized mannequins. For the twentieth year, Christmas trees will divide Park Avenue for sixty-two blocks with a band of light. At Herald Square, Macy's windows add an Eastern accent with some 200 animated figures, ranging from girls dancing in mosques (a practice not allowed by Moslems) to silk-garbed courtiers watching performing jugglers. Across the street its archrival, Gimbel's, counters with a real-life Santa who descends a wooden chimney every fifteen minutes, talks through a microphone to the kids on the street, and—of course—invites everyone inside."

For those who wanted to enjoy themselves indoors, there was a talent and culture boom in full swing. Cities had made a conscious effort to beef up their orchestras and support the arts. Christmas concerts and performances of Handel's *Messiah* became popular. And *The Nutcracker* ballet, which George Balanchine had revived in the 1950s, was now performed in almost every city in the country.

LIFE IN THE CORPS

There is no formal group for recovering ballerinas, but there probably should be. As a serious student of ballet for most of my youth, I came to dread the month of August. August meant that rehearsals for *The Nutcracker* were about to begin. It meant that for the next four months, I was going to hear Tchaikovsky, and lots of him.

Dancing *The Nutcracker* was the dream of every girl who ever got herself *en pointe*, and ballet being the competitive world it is, you do not say no. And so each year I would show up, limber up, and throw myself into rehearsals. Fortunately, the excitement and anxiety of opening night, along with the sheer exhilaration of performing, tamped down feelings of aversion, and I had made it through another year.

Several years ago, someone told me the story of another former dancer. She had ducked into Macy's with her boyfriend to do some holiday shopping. Suddenly, the music piped through the store switched to Tchaikovsky. Without a word to her beau, the dancer rushed off in search of an exit. When her boyfriend caught up with her outside, she uttered a single word— "Nutcracker"—with an expressive shudder. The story was relayed to me as an exaggeration of cnormous proportions. I, however, wasn't fooled. I believed every word.

—Kay Schuckhart

The Golden Age of Must See

For youngsters and those who preferred to stay home, TV throughout the 1960s offered a profusion of Christmas fare. Every drama and sitcom did a special show for the holiday, and beyond this there were specials. While there was a notable absence of memorable Christmas movies during the decade, television specials, for once, mostly lived up to their name.

During the 1960s, the team of Rankin and Bass produced a series of stop-animation features which included *Rudolph the Red Nosed Reindeer* (1964), *Cricket on the Hearth* (1967), and *The Little Drummer Boy* (1968). Popular as the shows were, they were eclipsed by two mega hits that arrived in the middle of the decade.

1961 ZENITH TV

New performance features, together with Zenith's famous handcrafted quality, give you the world's most carefree performance!

23" Zenith B&W (USA)
Model F3385H
$575.00

The Traveler. Magnificent French Provincial styling - authentic, from its gracefully tapered legs to the metallic corners, to its speaker panels. 23" Picture Window TV (282 square inches of rectangular picture area, 23" overall diagonal measurement). Sunshine® picture tube with Glare-Ban Screen. Space Command® remote control. Zenith's famous handcrafted chassis.

TVhistory.TV

Charles M. Schultz's *A Charlie Brown Christmas* originally aired on December 9, 1965 and became an instant hit. In Charlie Brown's wish to nourish a homely little tree until it shone with the true meaning of Christmas, and the characters' ultimate acceptance of each other's foibles, Americans saw values they feared were slipping away. Much the same could be said of the other classic of the era, Dr. Seuss's 1966 *How the Grinch Stole Christmas!*, which debuted the following year. Narrated by Boris Karloff, the story told of how one mean, green Grinch was foiled when the "powerless" citizens of Who-ville united to proclaim their belief in the goodness of the holiday. Like Charlie Brown's little tree, the Grinch was transformed by ordinary love and goodwill, values basic to most Americans.

And To All a Good Night

Over the decades, Christmases have come in good times and bad, in times of prosperity as well as times of want. They've come wrapped in swirls of excitement, and sometimes in clouds of worry and bittersweet longing. But through it all, beneath the glitter and the tinsel, Christmas has remained what it always was: a time to celebrate the joys of the world with the people we love most.

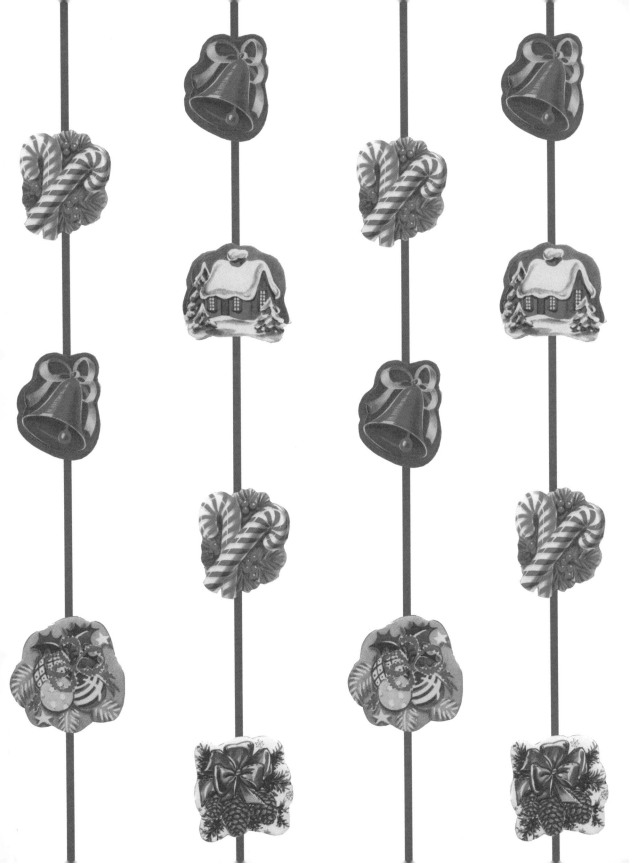

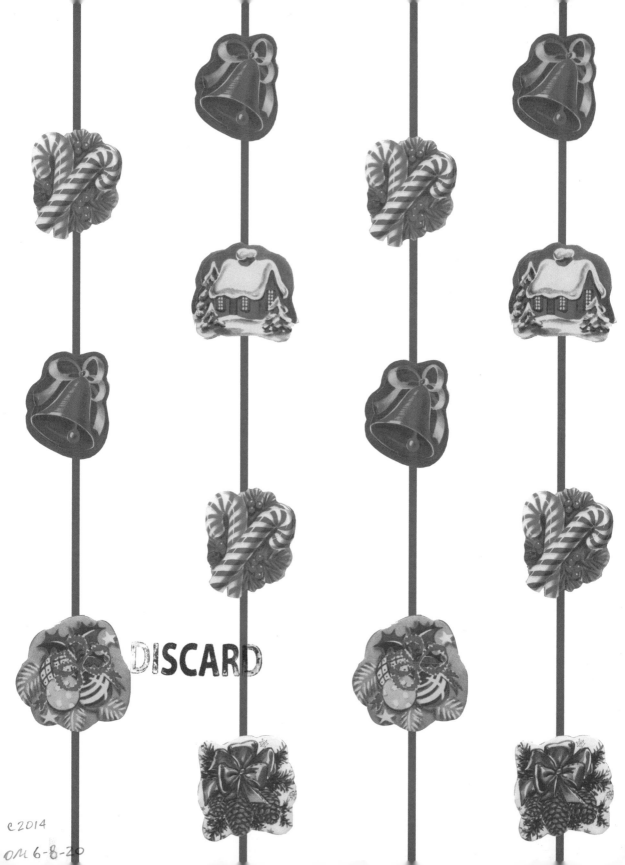

C 2014
OM 6-8-20